Bird Notes

Jane Mary Hayward

Printing Statement:

Due to the very old age and scarcity of this book, many of the pages may be hard to read due to the blurring of the original text, possible missing pages, missing text, dark backgrounds and other issues beyond our control.

Because this is such an important and rare work, we believe it is best to reproduce this book regardless of its original condition.

Thank you for your understanding.

BIRD NOTES

BY THE LATE

JANE MARY HAYWARD

EDITED BY EMMA HUBBARD

WITH FIFTEEN ILLUSTRATIONS FROM DRAWINGS BY G. E. LODGE
AND FRONTISPIECE

LONDON
LONGMANS, GREEN, AND CO.
AND NEW YORK : 15 EAST 16ᵗʰ STREET
1895

METEMPSYCHOSIS

OUT of the toil and trouble, out of the stream and
strife,
To the bosom of Mother Nature I now commend
my life ;
My torment and my treasure, I lay it down at her
feet,
The shadow and the sunshine, the bitter and the
sweet.
What will our Mother do with it ?   Whither away
will she fly ?
Will she play with it on the wavelets, or follow
the cloud through the sky ?
Will she fill the veins of the flowers, or dance
with it on the breeze ?
Will it swell the storm on the mountain, or the
murmur amidst the trees ?
Bury it not with the beetle, give it not to the
grass,
Where the heavy ox and the ploughman may
trample it as they pass ;
But, Mother O Mother of wonders ! — if ever a
prayer may be heard,
Let my poor little life spring upwards and beat in
the heart of a bird !

September 19, 1892.

The Sidmouth Garden

INTRODUCTION

A FEW words of introduction to this little book
are needed ; and they shall be but few, as neither
the incidents of the author's life, nor her feelings
towards publicity, would warrant more.

For many years I had asked my friend, Jane
Mary Hayward, to collect and publish her notes on
birds. I felt sure that the first-hand observations
of so sympathetic and unwearied a watcher would
have a value not to be measured by the limitations
of their scope. She, however, always doubted
whether they would have interest enough for any
wider circle than that of the friends who cared
for her, as well as for the birds and flowers that
counted for so much in her life. Sometimes she
was amused by the suggestion, and would perhaps
answer it in her next letter by a passage like the

following :—' It is all very well to talk of " pleasant fresh notes," but it is only because I am setting them down for you, who I know will care to read them, that they are pleasant and fresh ; and if I went to set them down book-wise, they would be anything but that. I should see before me we will say a great-grand-niece with an antiquarian turn, fingering superciliously an old yellow manuscript, very badly written, and remarking, " This was written by an ancient relative of mine ; an old maid who seems to have had nothing to do but to feed birds." Seriously, there is no reason to suppose that anyone would be interested The matter of anything I have to say—dealing, as it must deal, with individual birds, and not with birds in general—is so thin that it needs support.'

The first part, however, of these ' Bird Notes ' is the result of her taking a rather more favourable view of the possibility of putting them into permanent form ; a result aided by getting a notebook wherein to enter them. In a letter written about the time of this acquisition, after telling me that her nuthatches (who were always rather a source of difficulty in her bird community) were getting tamer and more civilised, and that she

began to like them better now that they pecked
less at the other birds, she says : ' Neither they
nor the other birds ever do anything that can be
recorded now that I have the note-book. However, I have written an introduction to the book
that is (not) to be, in which I have set down all I
remember of past bird-traits ; and have also found
a motto for the same, with which I am delighted.
It is from Monckton Milnes' poems :

" The World is large ; these things are small ;
They may be nothing—but they are all."

Don't you think it would be very appropriate ? '

' All ' they certainly were not to her ; though
only those who knew her well could realise how
much her life was enriched and cheered by the
never-failing interest of her bird companionship.

She had originally meant to devote her life to
the pursuit and practice of Art, and her father's
endeavours to secure good teaching for her brought
her into contact with Mulready, and afterwards,
through the introduction of their old friend, Miss
Mitford, of ' Our Village,' with Haydon the
painter. In some retrospective notes written in
1873 Miss Hayward says : ' We visited poor

Haydon in his studio a few years before his death by his own hand. He was wild in his manner then, and must certainly have been quite out of his mind when he penned the strange advertisements which appeared in the "Athenæum" and other papers just before the sad event.

'At the time we visited him he was painting David fighting the Lion, and his studio was strewn with the anatomical drawings that he had been making from the dissected body of a lion that had died in the Zoological Gardens. He had also just painted a large angel's head in fresco on the wall of his room. Fresco was then about to be reintroduced, as it was thought, and he was full of enthusiasm about it. Very much excited too! He had wounded himself just before by rushing against the point of a bayonet whilst painting a large picture of the Maid of Saragossa. He received us very kindly, and I was terribly shocked and grieved when I heard of his sad death.'

From this same book of retrospective notes I extract the following passage as showing something of the temper of mind of her early days, and as throwing light on the character of the verses that will be found among the Notes.

I believe I have always loved literature and knowledge more than Art, though I had longed to be a painter ever since reading Cunningham's "Life of Blake." How well I remember standing in the old shrubbery one bright warm summer morning, arresting myself under a Portugal laurel in a state of the wildest excitement, and panting, partly from the speed with which I had rushed there from the schoolroom where I had been reading, and partly with intense longing to paint, paint, paint—not anything visible in heaven or earth, but my fancies, as Blake did! I think it was reading that life that made me a painter.

'Well do I remember, too, the delight of reading some of Scott's works, and also his Life, under that same old Portugal laurel that I called my "Castle" in the days when we each had a tree-castle, from the top of which our flags floated. When I had finished Scott's Life, I put up a chalk monument to him under one of the fir-trees. I did it quite seriously, from a deep feeling of affection and reverence. And I did it *secretly*; that was characteristic. Any expression of emotion I was always curiously careful to conceal. For this reason I buried more than one early

"poem" under the fir-trees, or behind the root
house in the shrubbery—such was my horror and
fear lest they should be seen.   But I may as well

> " let fall
> The curtain of Oblivion o'er them all,"

as I said in some of those juvenile verses, which
I unfortunately buried where I could never find
them again, though they were enclosed for safety
in a tin pea-shooter!

'The dear old shrubbery!   As I look back, that
old shrubbery seems to me to be the very kernel
of my much-loved home.   At one time I almost
lived in it, never walking beyond it, except, on
Sundays, to church.   Its shades and silences, its
gleams and voices—now the murmur of the wind
in the tall Scotch firs, now the song of the many
birds all unconscious of my still presence—these
nourished the poetry of my life and taught me to
love solitude and meditation.   I sat there—knelt
there—again lately, under the old laurel, on the
sloping green-sward, when on a visit to the old
home which is no more mine.   " Not mine now!"
—it was a sad thought.   But as I sat and watched
the gleams of sunshine on the now green and

seldom-trodden paths, the conviction came to me
that it was mine still, mine only; that it was to
me what it never could be to any other; that its
influence had become part of my life; that its
heart was mine, and undiscoverable by any other.
So I took possession again, and enjoyed the
hour.'

To return to the 'Bird Notes.' They may be
thought in some degree to suffer from the lack of
any systematic plan that should connect and
arrange them in a more or less definite order; yet
this was never their aim, and their freedom and
freshness must have been dulled if they had been
written under the impression that they were to
be submitted to a possible circle of unknown
readers. They are a series of small sketches from
the life, jotted down by the writer at the moment
when the sight or sound was vividly present to
her senses; senses quickened by hereditary apti-
tude, by artistic training, and above all by that
loving sympathy which is the condition of true
insight.

Another objection too lies on the surface, and
an easy smile might be raised by the frank
'anthropomorphism' of many of the notes; yet

the smile would be misplaced, and perhaps on this head also more is gained than lost. Mr. Philip Hamerton remarks : 'The main difficulty in conceiving the mental states of animals is that the moment we think of them as *human* we are lost.' But there is a deeper insight in Mr. Lloyd Morgan's retort : '*Yes ; but the pity of it is that we cannot think of them in any other terms than those of human consciousness.* The only world of constructs that we know is the world constructed by man.' And it is just that 'reflex of a human face' always recognised by Miss Hayward in her favourites, that gives the clue and the interest to her account of their doings.

This fellowship with the birds lasted the whole of her life, and in her latest note to me, dated January 8, 1894—not a fortnight before her death—she says, ' L. has been in ; also a robin, formally introduced by Mrs. Halse' (her Devonshire servant) 'with, " Come along ! here's your Missus." '

The confidence of the birds as they waited on her window-sill, and watched their small 'Missus,' and clamoured for and enjoyed her gentle hospitality, was most remarkable : I never saw anything like it.

Her garden was not only a source of delight
to her, as long as she could work or even walk in
it, but it supplied her with subjects for her brush,
and her friends with many flowers and choice old-
fashioned plants. Botany, with its questions of
adaptation, of connection, of reversion, of protective
defence, was always of interest to her; and it was
to her that friends often turned for information or
suggestion in solving any botanical difficulty. In
this, as in other subjects, it was not the accumu-
lation of isolated facts that attracted her so much
as the large schemes of thought into which the
facts fitted—the lines of theory on which they
could be threaded in orderly sequence.

The verses are chosen from a large number in
my possession; they show but another branch of
that deep-rooted love of the beauty of the world
about her which was to her a tree of life.

Although the intention of making painting
the main occupation of her life was to a great
extent frustrated by ill-health, she still accomplished a good deal. Her brush was always at
the service of her friends, and she was often very
successful in giving the character of the head she
was painting. In 1853 she had no less than six

pictures hanging on the walls of the Royal
Academy. One of her best portraits was that in
oils of Professor F. D. Maurice, now in the
National Portrait Gallery. To those of us who
are old enough to recollect his preaching in
Lincoln's Inn Chapel, this portrait forcibly recalls
the pathetic, yearning expression of that noble
head.

In many directions Miss Hayward was a
woman of no common powers. She was a good
linguist; as a child keeping a diary in Italian, and
when she went from Wokingham in 1852 to live
in London, helping a friend who had started a
school for hurdy-gurdy boys, among whom many
dialects of Italian had to be spoken as well as
understood. At Sidmouth, besides amusing herself with many translations from German poets,
she was chosen as critic and judge by a small
Translation Society. And to help her understanding of the New Testament, she studied Greek.

But greater than her gifts in any special
branch of art or literature was her power of helping both head and heart of all those who enjoyed
the happiness of her friendship. The right book
would be given, the needful tools for carving or

modelling or painting would be found, the wise
suggestion would be ready, and the unstinted
wealth of loving sympathy would abound for the
many whom she loved. Her cares and anxieties
were so little concerned with self that in her later
years she was able with truth to write, 'All my
storms now are on other people's seas.'

Jane Mary Hayward was born at Wokingham January 26, 1825; and died at Sidmouth
January 20, 1894.

EMMA HUBBARD

THE VOICE OF AUTUMN

I SAID unto the Ocean, ' Speak thou for me, O Sea !
O restless, craving creature, thy voice shall speak for
    me !
Upon thy wind-lashed waters lift up my spirit's cry,
And bear it to the mighty cloud that sails along the
    sky ! '
But now, O voice of Autumn, that sigh'st amidst the
    trees,
'Tis thee I bid to speak for me and bear upon thy
    breeze
          To all I love a long farewell,
          A greeting, and a passing bell.

O gentle voice of Autumn, there is little else to say ;
My heart-beats old are well-nigh told, and I – I pass
    away.
Hope folded long ago her wings, and all desires are
    dead :
I only seek a resting-place for weary heart and head.
Yet speak for me a soft farewell to Nature's lovely face,
And cover with thy golden leaves my last long sleeping-
    place.
          To all I love, a long farewell,
          A greeting, and a passing bell.

ILLUSTRATIONS

BIRD NOTES

CHAPTER I

I LIVE alone, surrounded by fields and trees ; and the one large window of my quiet sitting-room looks across the top of a verandah on to a lawn and flower-beds full of roses, and full, therefore, of the aphides that birds love so well. An unfrequented road lies beyond that ; then a row of fine lime-trees and elms, a meadow, and a river. A Devonshire stream it is, that comes and goes in its red, rocky bed, with storm and sunshine ; sometimes thundering noisily over the weir ; sometimes murmuring dreamily amongst the flints that are brought down by freshets from the hills above ; and sometimes, here and there, hiding almost out of sight. A few days are sufficient to make the difference.

The graceful yellow wagtail loves our river, and the splendid grey one is often to be seen there. Both in summer and winter they haunt and

B

beautify it, and a delightful sight it is to see them chasing one another, or their shadows, from rock to rock, or playing with the water as they splash it all about them. The piebald one also abounds here, but it does not seem to care so much for the river ; it seems to prefer the roads and fields and even the house-tops. I have had one now and then upon my window-sill.

One day in autumn, some years ago, there was a curious sight : my lawn, and also the small lawns on either side, were covered with wagtails of all the three kinds, the piebald being, naturally, the most numerous. I never saw them collected in a flock before ; is it their custom ? and were they preparing for migration ? If so, I suppose the wagtails that we have here in the winter come to us from more northern countries. Flocks of larks and starlings have visited us in the same way when there has been much snow ; yet we have both birds with us during the winter as well as the summer. The larks, however, do not come down into the valley under ordinary circumstances. To hear *them* one must climb to the top of Salcombe Hill, which is 497 feet high, and very steep ; there they abound ; and there, too, may be heard the kitten-like cry of the plover. No ; when these poor larks visit us in such numbers, it is from a sad necessity ; the snow lies thick above

the frozen ground, and they are starving. Not a
blade of grass, not a green leaf of any description
that happens to be uncovered do they leave behind
them. It is a bad time for young plants of the
cabbage kind if they raise their heads at all above
the snow. Some of the larks probably cross the
Channel, or go west; but they are very weak, and
a large number fall a prey to hunger or the gun.

It is the same with the flocks of starlings;
they only make their appearance when quite
starved out. A piteous sight it is to see them
hammering desperately upon the iron earth—all
the more piteous because one cannot help them at
all. If food is placed before them they pay no
attention to it, but go on pecking the earth; or
perhaps they try to fly a little further—not far
though, they have not the strength. One snowy
winter, a few years ago, hundreds of them were
lying about dead in the fields, while others fell down
the chimneys into our rooms. Yet the starling
is a clever bird—a clever imitator, at all events.

There are some fine trees along the reach of
the river, just above the weir opposite to the
house; for the meadow on this side was once part
of the garden of Salcombe House, and is still
called 'The Lawn.' These trees are often full of
small birds: golden-crested wrens, and sometimes
goldfinches. More frequently there are tits of all

kinds, chiffchaffs, and whitethroats ; while plenty
of wrens and occasional coots haunt the bushes
below them. Sometimes a heron alights on the
marshy ground, through which a small rivulet
makes its way to the river ; sometimes a raven
flaps about in the boughs of the trees on the other
side ; but the yellow wagtail is there the constant
and never-failing delight.

Once, and once only, I started a blue kingfisher,
a pleasure I shall never forget. But that was
much higher up the river and in a much wilder
part ; it was far from any road or even path, and
at the upper end of the reach, overhung with trees
and bushes. I was searching the beds of flint in
the shallow water for a rare flower that I had
once found there, when the lovely creature rose
not many yards from me and flew straight away
up the stream, with a *slow and heavy* flight, as if
it really was a weight of jewels that flashed upon
its splendid back. I saw it alight on a bough
hanging over the water, and followed it up as well
as I could ; but the roughness of the way obliged
me to take my eye off it, and I lost it again.
Again I put it up further on, but I never saw it
so close and well as I could have wished.

Green woodpeckers are by no means rare birds
here. Strange and handsome creatures ! I
watched three feeding on my lawn one morning

in the small hours before the world was awake.
Birds have it all to themselves at that time, or, at
all events, they seem to think so; and so they
exhibit themselves and their manners and customs
with a delightful confidence. I had never seen
the green woodpecker before, and it was the sound
of a strange cry in the garden that aroused me
and made me go to the window. I was quite

GREEN WOODPECKERS

startled when I saw these three large strange-
looking birds plunging their bills into the ants'
nests, keeping them there a moment or two, then
withdrawing them with an air of satisfaction, and
again plunging them into the treasure-heap in such
a regular and business-like fashion; but I know
their form and fashions well now, for they often
pay my ants' nests a visit in the daytime, when

the day is wet and everything is more than usually quiet.

Owls abound here also, and much do I love to hear their weird cry at nights when the first frosts come ; but I have never had the good fortune to see one. A servant of mine, not remarkably truthful, I must admit, once told me that she had seen a row of small ones sitting on the garden wall when she opened the kitchen door one night. And once, when I was watching from dark to sunrise at an upper window, looking east, I saw what may have been an owl flitting away into the shades, just as things of light were beginning to arouse themselves.

There is a little grove of tall trees just within sight of my windows, and beyond 'The Lawn.' The river flows and sings over a shallow bed of flints most musically there, below the bank on which the trees stand, and on the opposite side are meadows and hedges. That is a capital place for watching birds. I have seen a flock of the large blackheaded tit there, but only once ; I do not think they flock together much. A handsome bird it is, but not graceful or interesting.

The reach of the river opposite these houses is, I think, the prettiest ; but there are other tree-bordered nooks and curves with pleasant meadow banks. How long, I wonder, will there be anything of the kind? Year after year there is less; I see it vanishing before my eyes. Directly the banks want repairing, trees are felled upon them, and laid beneath them to mend them. Why cannot trees be brought from some other place where they will not be missed? It may save trouble and expense for the moment to utilise these growing on the spot; but it is shortsighted, for, setting aside the loss of beauty, which the offenders are unable to appreciate, the roots of growing trees are the only things that can resist the rush of water. The dead ones laid under the bank are quickly destroyed and washed away.

And the curves of the river! Almost every year some tasteless riparian owner cuts straight some of its beautiful curves. Where is the lovely silver serpent that glided amongst the hills when I first came here? It is becoming something between a ditch and a canal for the greater part of its course as one sees it from the hills. Surely the natural beauty of a country is a valuable public property, one that ought to be guarded by the law, even at the expense of the landed proprietors, large or small. If the large landed proprietors will not be at the expense, nor take the trouble to preserve the beauty of their native country, which is, as it were, committed to their careless hands, their *raison d'être* ceases.

No doubt a fickle, riotous stream like this is difficult to keep in order; sometimes it tears down its own trees, but that is no reason why we should make matters worse instead of better.

Riotous it is indeed at times, and furious, and cruel! Three persons have been drowned in it since I came here. It was quiet when a poor old woman, nearly blind, walked into it in broad daylight, and was drowned, though there were houses near. It was a broad, boiling, devastating, storm-lashed torrent when a poor boy was blown off a foot-bridge into it before his father's face, and carried down so swiftly that rescue was impossible. That same night a poor woman, half mad, who lived in a cottage near it, was left for a few minutes by the son and husband who had been told to watch, and who only left the house to secure something threatened by the wind, and away was she—out into the storm and darkness, and into the boiling rushing flood and the darker gulf of eternity! No doubt the nerve-storm was at its height in her poor frame also. I have known such coincidences before.

Those who study the connection between storms in the sun and magnetic storms, the aurora borealis and allied phenomena, would do well to take the nerve-storms into consideration also. I am persuaded that they are closely connected, and that much might be learnt from the connection.

THE RIVER

O! the green pellucid river,
Where the sunbeams dance and quiver;
Dance and quiver, fling and float,
Merrily to the blackbird's note!

O! the green pellucid river,
Where the sunbeams shake and shiver;
Shake and shiver, shrink and fly
From a thing that there doth lie —

From a thing that lieth there,
Pond-weed tangled in its hair;
Helpless hands washed to and fro,
As the careless currents flow.

From the fixed and stony eye
Duck and dipper frightened fly;
Whilst the river as it flows
Hoarsely whispers what it knows—

What it knows and what doth keep
In its hollows dark and deep;
Whilst, above, the sunbeams quiver
On the smoothly smiling river.

CHAPTER II

MORE than fifteen years have passed away since I first began to provide a morning meal at my window for the birds; and I have derived a large amount of amusement and interest from the practice, and also not a little instruction. One of the first things that I learnt was the great resemblance between birds and children; and the discovery has been of great use in dealing with them. No doubt we are all of a piece, their little wills and ways are the result of balanced instinct; the same instincts, and as nicely balanced, as those of babies. A little more hunger, a little less fear; a little less hunger, a little more fear; up and down goes the balance with unerring regularity, modified only by the state of the weather and the different characters of the different species of birds.

The action of a blue tit spreading its wings over a nice little heap of crumbs that it wishes to keep all to itself, scolding all the while at any other bird that attempts to approach, is so like that of a covetous and angry child spreading its

WINTER TIME

little fat arms over its toys that one can but laugh
at it. One ought perhaps rather to sigh than to
laugh to find so many unpleasant human qualities
in such pretty little beings; but I love my birds,
and laugh at them. *My* birds. I do not exactly
know what right I have to call them *my* birds;
my property in them is slight if any. But I do
not wish for more. I would not have a bird in a
cage for the world: it would be a perpetual torture
to me until I let it out. I do not even wish to
tame them; I have a dread of their becoming too
tame, lest it should make them careless of danger.
I wonder what became of the dear little robin that
followed me about in the garden last autumn, and
came at my call, and even, once, took crumbs from
my hand? I did not tame it; it presented itself
at my feet one day, quite tame; and immediately
accepted the situation of under-gardener, sure to
be at hand if I began to stir the earth, or turn out
a plant from a flower-pot, and ready to relieve me
of any unfortunate worm or insect that came to
the surface. And O how quick it was to see
them! I turned round one day to see why the
bird had suddenly hopped away from me, and
behold! it had a large spider in its mouth,
struggling and kicking. And it forthwith swallowed the same, struggles and all. It was a large
spider, but the bird must have had wonderful eyes

to see it so far off as it did. I really believe that
that little robin—a young one, I think—loved *me*
as well as my crumbs. It always came to meet
me when I went into the garden if it was there,
or came to my call if it was in the next garden.
But one day I called in vain. Only the day before
it had hopped up to me in the most lively and
affectionate manner; but that day, and every day
after, I called in vain! It was a sad business.
What became of it? Was it cat or dog or trap
that deprived me of my pet? Or was it the
jealousy of some older and stronger robin? I am
inclined to think that the latter was the cause;
and that an older and bolder robin (bolder towards
birds, not towards me), that appeared in the
garden about that time may have chased the tame
one away. I am the more inclined to think this,
first, because the tame one was very much afraid
of other robins, and immediately sought the
shelter of a bush if it heard the note of one in the
distance, and also because the same thing happened
once before, some years ago. In that case also
the robin presented itself at my feet one day
without any invitation on my part, and it seemed
to me that it was aiming at the shelter of my
dark brown dress. It was a very timid bird, and
seemed seldom to leave the shelter of a bush
except to come to me. A frightened creature

naturally seeks the protection of something of like
colour to itself : a blue tit flies to the top of a tree,
to the green leaves and blue sky—so does the
nuthatch ; a robin seeks the brown shade of a
bush or laurel—so does a blackbird.   Of this I
am sure, as I have had abundant opportunities of
observing it at my window ; and so I cannot help
thinking that this young robin may well have felt
some comfort and security in the proximity of my
dark red-brown dress.   But alas ! it was a false
security ; for one day, when it was at my very
feet, an angry and jealous robin, after scolding
it violently from the top of a wall, dashed down
upon the poor little thing in the most savage
manner ; and, after a flying fight in the air which
I was helpless to prevent, drove it away.   I saw
it two or three times afterwards ; but it soon
left.

It is a mystery to me why some robins should
be so strangely tame and some so savage.   Is it
perhaps against robin-law that a member of the
community should seek human fellowship and
crumbs ?   Is it that the hen robin has an ear but
no voice, and is attracted by the human voice, as
it is by that of its own kind ?   Or is it that the
younger birds have to be taught to be afraid of
danger, and that the savage attack of the older
robin was merely a severe lesson ?   Whether

taught or not, they certainly learn it from the older birds; the fear does not come altogether naturally to them: I have had many proofs of this. Two young chaffinches were almost brought up upon my window-sill last spring. They underwent a regular course of instruction in the art of eating, and most amusing it was to watch it. At first not a crumb was taken without the assistance of a parent bird; gradually they were left a little more, and when the pinch of hunger was strong they would try to peck up a little for themselves, crying all the time. Directly the parents came back their helplessness also returned, and the large mouths gaped and the wings drooped entreatingly. A most voracious bird was one of them—the son and heir, and such a little Turk! He would not suffer any bird not of the family to come upon the window-sill while he was there. It was absurd to see how birds much more powerful than himself retreated before the open-mouthed attack of the courageous young thing that could not yet feed itself. I noticed that though the parents flew away when I went too close to the window, the young ones at first merely looked round in astonishment, and then began to peck about for the crumbs. After a time they also flew away if I went too near.

I noticed the same thing when some long-

tailed tits visited me one winter. They had no
idea of being afraid of anything on the other side
of the window: possibly they could not see me.
I think the smaller birds have great difficulty in
seeing through a window. I could put my head
quite close to them without frightening them.
But they noticed the fear of the other birds, and
after some time—some weeks—followed their
example and flew away too.

The robin seems to see further into a room
than any other bird (it sees me as I sit by the fire),
but with that exception the rule seems to be that
the larger the bird—the larger its head, that is—
the more easily it sees me through the window.
The cole tit seems to see further than the blue tit;
but then, though its body is smaller, its head and
eye are, I think, rather larger. The blue tit does not
see far, and it usually refuses to be alarmed until it
really does see for itself the cause of the sudden
flight of the other birds. A very funny thing it is
to see a blue tit stand on end, as it were, and peer
over into the room on tiptoe, drawn out to its
thinnest and longest, and then, either not seeing me
or thinking that I am not dangerous, settle down
comfortably into a little round ball in the midst of
the crumbs, only too glad to get them all to itself.
Very greedy and very courageous is the blue tit;
plebeian and ungraceful in manner, but of all birds

the most comical and amusing. It is by far the
most common bird on my window-sill during the
winter, but in the summer it goes further afield.
I had, however, once a curious proof that it does
not lose sight of its winter resources, and that it
retains a certain sense of property in them. It
was thus. One day in September I was standing
at the window, which was closed, when to my
great satisfaction I saw a long-tailed tit in the
garden below, a bird I had not seen for a long
time. I saw it come nearer and nearer until it
alighted upon a rose-branch that rises above the
top of the verandah, and forms a pretty and convenient perch. But just as I was hoping that it
might come a little nearer, and alight upon the
window-sill, down came two blue tits upon it
and began bustling about and pecking away at the
bare stone just as if it had been covered with
crumbs. Now there were not only no crumbs
there, but there had not been any for many
months, and there could be no other possible
interpretation of this curious little scene than
that these were two old *habitués* come to claim
their own feeding-place to the exclusion of long-
tailed tits and all other invaders, and the sense of
property was so strong in them that they took
not the slightest notice of my presence close to
the window, of which they must have been aware.

The long-tailed one allowed the claim and gracefully flew away, to my great regret.

There appears to be a great antagonism between these two species of tit. I saw one day what seemed to be a pitched battle going on between two little armies of them in some larches, of which tree there is a small wood further up the river. In that case the blue tits were driven off, or at all events they took to flight *en masse*, and left the others in possession. But O the chattering and fluttering there was about it!

Most birds seem to be afraid of the sharp bills and the resolution of the blue tit. I have seen robins, sparrows, chaffinches, and even the nuthatch fly before it. A very spirited little bird is the graceful long-tailed tit ('bottle-tits,' as we called them in Berkshire, from the form of their exquisite nest), very lovely, and withal aristocratic-looking; the blue tit looks extremely plebeian beside it. Alas, since the bitter winter of three or four years ago, I have seen but few of them. The golden-crested wren too has become very scarce since then. The long-tailed tits are not birds that frequent the neighbourhood of houses much, but flocks of them—families, I should say, of ten or twelve—used formerly to pass through my garden now and then, lingering and flitting among the trees.

Once, soon after I came here, when this house was surrounded by old orchards and fields and hedges, I had a great treat. The winter was severe and thick snow covered both the ground and the trees. Besides strewing crumbs on the window-sill above, I had placed some on a flower-stand under the verandah below, just before the dining-room window. I was sitting in the drawing-room above when a flute-like note drew me to the window, and I saw in the garden below a bird that was strange to me. I went downstairs to get a nearer view of it, and to my great delight found about a dozen lovely little long-tailed tits feeding upon the flower-stand! They took complete possession that winter not only of the flower-stand but of the window-sill above. They would wait in the morning in the trees opposite (I could hear their clear, flute-like notes as I was getting up), and as soon as I closed the window after putting out the crumbs for them, down they would fly with an undulating motion, like a flight of arrows, straight to me. I almost felt as if I were going to be shot, but apparently they did not see me at all behind the glass, and would begin to feed at once. Most lovely little things they were, with such graceful, high-bred manners. Very sociable too; if one of them happened to come alone at any time (and they came and went all

day long), it would not eat till it had piped up a
companion to eat with it. In order to accommo-
date so many long tails in so confined a space,
they would stick them almost straight up into the
air to be out of each other's way. One evening, I
remember, when it was getting dark, a little thing
came alone and piped for a long time without
being able to make any of its companions hear.
It took no notice of me, though I put my face
close to it. At last I began to think it would stay
all night, and was wishing I could open the
window without alarming it, and take it in, when
all in a moment it was gone; I suppose it at
last heard a voice in the distance answering it. I
believe they sleep closely clustered together on a
bough side by side, and probably could not sleep
otherwise. No doubt union is warmth to them, if
not strength. Perhaps it is strength too; though
so small, they never seem afraid when all together.
Very gentle birds they are, but I did once see one
defy a blue tit, and very pretty its anger was. The
blue tits, though they had not at that time made
themselves so much at home as they did afterwards, were not at all kind to them. I was
obliged sometimes to play the policeman among
them, and to protect the delicate little long-tailed
tits from the others. This I was able to do
because the blue tits could see me when the others

could not; so, if I heard any quarrelling going on,
I went near enough to the window for the blue tits
to see a warning finger held up to them, when
they speedily dispersed, leaving the longtails
wondering but happy. They remained in the
neighbourhood till late in the spring, and indeed
in the summer I once caught sight of one on the
sill as I came into the room; the window was
open, and it saw me, and vanished in a moment,
though not before I had seen that it had a new
light summer dress on.

The one bird that never altogether leaves me
is the chaffinch. It is coarse and plebeian in
appearance and voice and manner (it appears to
me to have a 'cerebral r' in its voice); it eats even
more than the sparrow, and drives away the other
birds if it can; but its extreme tameness is taking,
and there is a great deal of beautiful colour about
it. The soft browns of the hen bird please me
more than the bolder tints of the cock, and I think
she is the tamer of the two. One old hen chaffinch
was incessantly here all last spring and summer.
I seldom put any crumbs out, but she came all the
same, and did not move though I put my face
close to the window. One day we had this little
conversation in the words of Browning: "'What,
and is it really you again?' quoth I. 'I again?
what else did you expect?' quoth she." She said

it plainly to my eye, with the little impertinent
head well thrown back and all on one side, and
looking straight at me. I laughed, but she did
not go. No, they are not interesting birds, but it
is an advantage that you can distinguish the cock
and hen, and also, to some extent, the old and
young; and I cannot forget the confiding way in
which that old lady and her husband brought their
son and daughter to be fed and taught to feed
upon my window-sill last spring.

The nuthatch is a very amusing bird, with a
great deal of character, as one would imagine it
likely to have, with its curious figure, and its fine
large dark inquiring eyes. They do not come
every winter, but this winter they have been very
constant visitors in the morning. Though they
take it, they do not seem to care much for bread;
but I put out scraps of bacon after breakfast, and
then there is immense excitement among them:
they dare anything and everything for it, sending
all the other birds to the right about, and looking
me boldly in the face. One—there are only two
that come, I think—seems rather afraid of the
other, and is rather smaller, and not quite so bold.
I have however seen them, with lance in rest,
ready to fly at each other. Their appetite for
bacon seems to be unappeasable; they pack their
large beaks full, and bustle off with it, and are

back again for more in an incredibly short space
of time. I believe they store it.

The little cole tit timidly bides its time upon a
rose-branch, and when the nuthatch goes, up it
comes for a little bit, snaps it up nervously and is
away with it at once. Those who stay to feed do
it circumspectly, they are so afraid of the long
sharp beak of the nuthatch. It is difficult to
frighten a nuthatch; if I am too close it will hang
on for a moment with its claws to the edge of the
sill, and look sagely at me as if to ask leave. It
swings its long beak and large head to and fro all
the time, as if it wished to examine circumstances
on all sides, and, if possible, to see behind my
head; then, seizing three or four large pieces at
once, away it goes. But though tame and amusing,
there is something in its flat figure and sprawling
legs that I dislike; it is almost reptilian. I am
afraid too that it is a cruel bird and dangerous to
the others, judging by the savage stabs with which
it sometimes attacks them, and their fear of it. I
think I must lay to its charge the untimely death
of a poor little chaffinch that I found dead below
the window-sill one day, with a hole in its skull.
I know that the nuthatch had been feeding and
fighting there in the morning whilst I painted
behind my curtain; and I heard once a shrill cry,
and a flap of feathers against the window. When

I looked out there was nothing to be seen; but there was death below—a murder had been committed!

That is not the only tragic occurrence I have witnessed here. One day—a day of frost and deep snow—I found a little blue tit on the verandah, dead, and almost buried in the snow. I drew it up, hoping that life might not be quite extinct; but I could not restore it. Sometimes birds have come with broken or dangling legs, or with only one—a sad sight that! One came thus for two years, but generally such a disadvantage in the struggle for life must tend to bring it to a speedy conclusion. A one-legged robin came at one time, but not for long. An old hedge-sparrow lived for many years in the garden with its head quite bare of feathers, and apparently very feeble on the wing. It was a sweet singer and very tame, but it never came to my window. When I last saw it, it was lying on its side on the lawn in a sunny spot, lifting up its wing to expose its old side to the comfort of the sunshine. A simple gentle bird is the hedge-sparrow, and very tame sometimes; and its song, though weak and wiry compared with some, is very pleasant; it is so peaceful. Besides, it sings on when all other birds are silenced except the robin.

'Except the robin.' How often one has to say

that ; what a very exceptional bird it is in many
ways, and how much more our own ! He has a
property in us too, at all events in our gardens and
homes. And he knows it : a full-grown robin
seems to have a quite singular sense of property
in a garden ; he will not, if he can prevent it, allow
any other robin to come into the particular
enclosure that he considers his own. He also
objects to *unusual* birds of other kinds. I have
often been called to the window by the excited
warning note of the robin, and have found, sometimes indeed a cat, but more often an invasion of
unusual birds of a more or less interesting kind—
a flock of chiffchaffs, a passing company of long-
tailed tits or golden-crested wrens, or a goldfinch
or even a greenfinch ; for the latter seldom comes
here, or the yellowhammer either, though both I
think are common on the hills and higher up the
valley. Even the marsh tit is sufficiently a stranger
to excite the indignant jealousy of the robin.

Greenfinches were frequently here in the
autumn at one time ; but that was when I had a
tall and widely spreading sweet-briar in the middle
of the kitchen garden. The abundant fruit of this
tree attracted them, and very handsome they
looked—quite splendid indeed—poised on the
long arched and swinging branches covered with
scarlet hips.

Once only have I seen a bullfinch here, and that did not come to the window. Neither do the wrens come, though there are plenty about : twice only have I seen one for a minute on my window-sill. Goldfinches never come to the window, but I used to see them frequently at one time, and

BULLFINCH

once a pair took it into their gay little heads to build in a sycamore close by. I saw those birds once more, only once. I caught sight of them one day flying about a yellow honey-suckle on the wall near their old home, and they seemed about to build in it : this they very wisely did not do.

After all it is as perilous to place one's love too low as too high. I was grieved to lose those goldfinches.

A chaffinch too in my garden has apparently had the same object, that of protection by means of colour, in view. Its nest, in a juniper, is made of bright moss, exactly the tint of the young shoots of the tree. This, I am sorry to say, appears to have been abandoned. There were several eggs in it, which were quite cold when I found it.

Besides protective colouring there are two other qualities that recommend certain materials to nest-builders, viz. flexibility and length. Every-one must have noticed how sparrows and other birds will steal pieces of string or thread, or any-thing long and limp, when they are building. Only the other day I caught a sparrow trying hard to untie a piece of thick string by which the branch of a tree had just been tied back; it would have succeeded if I had not come to the rescue. I have had the ties of budded roses taken away by them also. I have seen forget-me-not, alyssum, laburnum, and clematis, all long and limp sprays, made use of. Rooks too are fond of young branches of weeping willow. But there can be no doubt that birds have a very keen sense of the protectiveness of colour; if a blue tit is startled, it is sure to take refuge in a high branch against the sky—blue and brown and green. A robin flits away to the brown shadow of a bush. A thrush, as soon as it is born, is wonderfully clever in finding its own tints on some wall or tree-trunk. It makes believe to be a piece of this to such an extent that one may approach quite close to it, and it will remain absolutely motionless, so long as one's eye is upon it. If the eye is removed, even for a 'twinkling,' the bird will have disappeared silently behind something before one can look again.

A pair of sparrows in the garden some time ago showed much ingenuity and perseverance. They began a nest in a Pyrus japonica against this white house. I removed it, not wishing for the noise and dirt so near the window ; they began again, and again I had it removed. This time, although it was apparently little more than a flat beginning, there were eggs upon it, so I suppose they had made it as small as they could, to avoid observation. They tried again, and on removing it the third time I found that the birds were overlaying it with the white flowers of some sweet alyssum growing below, as if from a wish to render it less conspicuous against the white house. The flowers were quite fresh and numerous. After this they made two more trials—five in all —and the last time the attempted nest was

almost entirely made of white alyssum. I got a
dreadful scolding whenever I went near the place,
but after the fifth attempt they gave it up. Last
year they tried the same thing, and I removed
two nests; I however allowed a thrush that had
built below to remain, and bring up its brood there.
After the thrushes were gone, the sparrows immediately built on the top of the forsaken thrush's
nest! They seem to have drawn the conclusion,
rather too hastily but not irrationally, that that
must be a safe place for them. I do not know
that their thoughts took the shape of words, but
they chattered over it immensely, and I do not
know where the line can be drawn between words
and exclamations, nor between those and the cries
of birds, which are more varied and numerous
and distinctive in purpose than is generally imagined.

It may be said that there is no progress nor
addition to the language of birds; but I am not
sure of this. Last winter a robin, accustomed to
be fed on my window-sill with bits of bacon,
invented a note by which it called me to the
window to feed it. It was a quite peculiar note,
hushed, muttered, short; the object seemed to be
to reach my ear and not that of rival birds. I
always found it waiting for the opening of the
window and putting out of the food; it would

CHIFFCHAFF FEEDING YOUNG CUCKOO

then take a very few little bits, look gratefully
into my face, and fly away till it was hungry again,
then *da capo*. The same robin hops in and out
now continually through the open window, and
takes what it pleases.

I saw a strange sight lately in the garden of
the next house from an upper window of my own.
A young cuckoo had alighted on the top of a stake,
and was loudly and hoarsely crying for food. The
other birds seemed to be all flying away from it
in alarm ; but suddenly a very small one, a chiffchaff I think, flew straight to the cuckoo, and after
fluttering about its head like a moth, popped
something into its mouth, and then flew away for
more. The cuckoo looked large enough to swallow
its foster-parent, and was strong on the wing, and
apparently full-grown.

I have been watching the soaring of the
martins, who seem to be obliged to attain a certain height before they can cross the Channel.
During the late prevalence of north-east winds
large flocks might be seen going across in a south-
westerly direction. One day, while I was watching
a flock crossing in this direction at a great height,
I was puzzled by seeing a number of them below
flying round and round, and about and over and
even below the trees with a general inclination of
flight in the opposite direction. At last I made

D

up my mind that they were breasting the wind
in order to rise upon it, kite-like, to the necessary
height. Another day I watched from the cliff a
small flock performing the same manœuvres, but
as the wind was north-west, they took a course
over the sea which seemed, as far as I could trace
it, to be south-east. Do they rise till they can
see the opposite coast? or do they find a stronger
wind at that height to help them?

I have often watched gulls rising in that way
on the wind. Very greatly they seem to enjoy it,
and they apparently have no object in it but en-
joyment. Till the wind masters them, there is
not the slightest motion of the wings to be seen.

STILL the same, ever the same, this outward face of
    things !

Time but toucheth it gently—little the change it
    brings.

Here, where we sat together, spreadeth the self-same
    tree,

Curved and matted the branches, just as they used to
    be.

Even the rich-toned lichen keepeth its place and form,

Mellowing the old grey oak-bark, tinting it sunset-
    warm.

Grandly the dome of beech-trees archeth the old wood
    o'er ;

Vividly fretteth the sorrel the deep brown beech-leaf
    floor.

Even the delicate flowers cling to the same old spot ;

Meadow-sweet decks the river, and blue forget-me-not.

Close to the feathery larch-tree the woodbine clingeth
    still ;

Sweet is the rose in the valley, golden the gorse on
    the hill.

Cruel, cruel Nature ! tear off the treacherous veil !

Away with the smile of mockery ! tell us a truer tale !

Shatter the painful image of changeless trees and
    stones ;

Thou art a whited sepulchre, all full of mouldering
    bones !

But the solemn voice of Nature rose on the wind and
    said :

' Why wilt thou still be seeking the living amidst the
    dead ? '

D 2

CHAPTER III

January 1, 1882.

A STRANGELY warm winter this has been, so far. I have had fewer birds upon my window-sill in consequence of it. Not, indeed, fewer of my ordinary visitors: blue tits, cole tits, nuthatches, sparrows and chaffinches—of these I have plenty; but last year the larger birds, thrushes and black-birds, and even starlings, were glad to come. But then last year the snow was deeper than I have ever known it; it covered everything eatable, and the birds seemed to eat, or to try to eat, anything they could get. I saw a blackbird, after three ineffectual attempts, swallow one of the large frozen hips of the Scotch rose: it must have been like swallowing a marble. How any birds, except those that were fed, survived that winter I cannot think. This year it is just the reverse; we have had no snow and scarcely any frost. Gales, indeed, there have been, many and violent; and torrents of rain, but no real winter.

To-day I heard the fully developed spring note

of the blue tit. I heard it a little on December 27,
but it was then only tentative; now it is the
perfect trill, clear though short. I do not think I
ever before heard it so early. The blue tit has
several quite distinct notes; and besides that, the
tone of its notes varies a good deal. From its
being so much more constantly on the window-
sill than any other bird, I have learnt to understand its language better.

Generally, while I am at breakfast, there are
three or four of them at a time, picking up the
minute remains of the crumbs of the day before
(their regular breakfast succeeds mine), and
keeping up all the time a pretty little contented
twitter which tells me that no larger bird is there.
Suddenly there is a change of tone which a less
accustomed ear might perhaps not notice; I look
out carefully, and there is a chaffinch or some
other intruder—perhaps another tit, which they
think one too many for the crumbs. The discon-
tented tone increases, and is accompanied by
equally expressive irritated gestures, till at last
there is a savage attack which, from its sudden-
ness, nearly always sends away the stronger bird.
The small beak too of the blue tit is probably
nearly as sharp as a needle. Sometimes the dis-
contented tone only ends in the *scolding note*.
This is a very distinct note, and quite unmis-

takable. If I hear it in the garden I feel sure
there is a cat about, or perhaps a marsh tit, or
one of the large blackheaded tits, or some other
bird that is not often there, and that is therefore
considered an intruder.

I was myself severely scolded once by a golden-
crested wren. I was standing by the dining-room
window, which was closed, watching the pretty
little thing. It flitted to and fro, and twisted in

GOLDEN-CRESTED WREN

and out of the branches of a rose-tree growing
close to me, up the column of the verandah.
Suddenly it saw me, saw me in most alarming
proximity. But instead of at once flying away, it
put up its golden crest, clung fast to its twig, and
scolded. It was something between a hiss and a
groan—or rather grunt ; in miniature of course,
but I felt it deeply. You laugh ? It is perfectly
true, I assure you. A dog knows when it is being

laughed at, and does not like it; why should not I know when I am being scolded by a golden-crested wren, and feel it also? I was very much grieved; the more so that the little thing flew away afterwards, and left me lamenting.

The warning note of any bird seems to be understood by all; at all events that of the robin is, and being a watchful keen-sighted bird, with a loud sharp cry, it often acts as watchman to the others. I have frequently seen a bird that was feeding quietly at the window, unaware of my presence at the other side of it, turn sharply round on hearing the warning note of the robin, and look about for the danger; but the bird, especially if it is a blue tit, will not fly away till it has itself seen the source of danger, and even then, if very hungry, it will sometimes just turn its back on me and go on feeding industriously. Birds seem to fear danger less than fear itself; they do not like to be startled. And the little birds' hearts beat so quickly! Any one who has ever taken one in his hand must know that; they seem all nerves. I watched a hungry little blue tit the other day when the wind was shaking the window, at every click the little thing started and opened its wings, but it was not really afraid; it did not leave its crumbs.

Birds faint easily I have heard—was it faint-

ness or fear of the depth below that made a robin
hang back in my hand one day when I had caught
it while beating itself against the window of a
room on the third story, and was putting it out
of the same? Robins are hardly birds of the air,
and though they like the top of a wall, or the
peak of a low gable, they are seldom seen on high
trees ; and this robin may have felt dazed and
awed for a moment by the height from which it
had to descend. When it did so its swift oblique
flight was little short of a fall with a parachute.

January 4, 1882.

What a jealous bird the robin is ! or is it from
pride that it scarcely ever comes to the window
to feed with the other birds? It comes indeed in
very cold and frosty weather ; but it seems, even
then, to do it under protest ; there is a flash of
the bright eye and an indignant pose and turn of
the head which are very amusing, and express
very plainly that the other birds are far beneath
him and that no one has any right there but himself ; all of which is sometimes even more plainly
expressed by a stab with the beak. I have seen a
robin lower his lance, as it were, to run at a nuthatch, and even at a blackbird. The nuthatch is
feared by all more than any other bird ; I have
seen a chaffinch defy one, but then the nuthatch

had his tremendous beak well stuffed with bread ;
he lowered it nevertheless, but both thought
better of the matter, and there was no fight.

This morning when I opened the window I
saw a robin hopping about below, and I called it,
as mellifluously as I could ; it hopped towards
me, and looked up, and seemed inclined to come ;
but a chaffinch at that moment settled on the
verandah, and away went the robin at once. It
cannot be fear that keeps it away ; for, as I said
before, it fears none of them, and can rout the
whole company if necessary.

I think, therefore, it must be some kind of
supercilious feeling. Perhaps it has some right to
this feeling ; it stands more upright than the
other small birds, has a larger and more far-
seeing eye, a more lively motion than most, and
a much more varied note and sensitive ear. It is
an enthusiastic musician. Last autumn I was
made curiously aware of the sensitiveness of its
ear. I do not think my voice is particularly
enchanting, but I found that while working in
my garden, with a robin as my companion not far
off, I could make it come to me, or fly close past
me, by softly saying, ' Bob, Bob, Bob, pretty little
Bob ! ' and so on, for some time ; but I also found
that if I was at all hoarse I could make no impression. The charm for the robin was gone with

the softness of the tone; the bird seemed to feel
the difference as much as I did.

I think the robin must have inherited the
notion that its name is Bob, and that it is the
bird beloved by man. It is certainly better fitted
to be his companion than the other small birds;
it catches the invitation in the human eye more
readily, and understands man better. I had a
duet with a robin lately. I 'bob-bob-bobbed' my
sweetest, and he, sitting overhead in a bay-tree,
answered each time with an elaborate strain
which seemed to be never twice the same.
Whether it was intended to eclipse mine or to
respond to it I cannot say, but the bird seemed
delighted, and was so much excited that he
appeared ready to hop down upon me.

I feel sure that among the birds themselves
there is competitive singing. I have often heard
two and even three robins, perched on different
garden-walls and answering each other, each time
with a different strain, and evidently trying to
outdo each other. I have also seen a blackcap
and a whitethroat sing at each other, perched on
two boughs of the same tree. Each appeared to
be trying to sing the loudest, till at last they flew
at each other, like two angry dogs. Sometimes I
have thought that the duet between two robins
has been a singing-lesson, and that the less capable

bird was a young one, trying to imitate its
parent.

January 11, 1882.

I think that the singing of the blackbirds and
thrushes is exceptionally fine here. Perhaps it is
because there are no nightingales to rival them
and put them out of countenance. I remember

THRUSH BREAKING SNAILS

it was the same in Leicestershire, where also there
were no nightingales. Perhaps—and more likely
—because there is such a large provision of snails
for them in the old stone walls, and under the
lush foliage of this valley. Slugs also abound;
but do they eat the slugs? I fear not.

A few days ago I turned over a piece of slate
that had been lying for some time in the kitchen

garden, and behold, it was a mass of snails on the
lower side. There must have been two or three
score of them of all sizes. I had them taken to
a safe distance from the garden, and there they
were left to the thrushes ; but they were so firmly
glued down to the slate that I doubt whether a
thrush would have the power to raise them. I do
not think a thrush could break the shell of an old
snail without raising it and hammering it against
some hard substance. I found a flower-pot
saucer one day that a thrush had almost filled
with snail-shells—it had made use of it as an
anvil, in fact. Is not an anvil a tool? If so,
then thrushes make use of tools. If it is *not*,
then I suppose a tool is something held in the
hand ; but no sharp line can be drawn between
using the hand, or nail, or claw, and using something held in the hand. Any way, I think one
may say that the thrush made use of my saucer
as a tool wherewith to break its snail-shells. Very
good use it made of it too—good for the garden
as well as for itself and family.

January 12, 1882.

I wonder what the large birds are that I have
been watching from the beach this afternoon. A
fisherman whom I questioned afterwards thought
they must have been swans. But they were quite
black against dark clouds, and therefore could

hardly have been swans, unless the black swan
has ceased to be a *rara avis*. There were only
two when I first remarked them, but several
others joined them afterwards. They were flying
at some height, and apparently were about to
cross over to France, but all at once they stopped
and wheeled round and round over the sea, ascend-
ing higher every time, as if they wished to get a
sight of some distant destination. They did not,
however, go off in any direction, but mounted
higher and higher, on the wings of the wind as
it seemed, for their own were outspread in almost
motionless majesty, till they were nearly out of
sight. The clouds stretched in a long perspective
of ever-nearing lines to within a short distance
of the horizon, where they terminated in curtains
of purple and gold, through which some splendid
mystery seemed trying to break. The sea was
grand and gloomy, and corresponded well with the
spectacle of these large, black, long-necked birds
with arched and pointed wings, whose magnificent
and ever-ascending gyrations seemed to symbolise
the human soul, for ever striving upwards towards — a canopy of clouds !

Birds of passage assemble here before crossing
the Channel. I have often watched them making
use of the wind by flying against it to raise themselves to the necessary height, as a kite is raised.

The consequence of this is that they often appear,
when the wind is off shore, to be trying to fly
inland again. A very beautiful sight it is to see a
large gull *slide down* the wind, as one does sometimes. It turns to leeward at a great height, and
seems then to abandon itself to the conflicting or
combined forces of gravity and the wind, which
carry it, without one flap of the wings, far out of
sight in a slow and majestic oblique descent.
There are few things in nature more beautiful
than the motion of a gull.

January 24, 1882.

Why are sparrows and chaffinches so much
more afraid of a white plate than the other birds
are? I have been putting enticing little bits of
bacon on such a plate lately, apart from the bread,
for convenience sake, and have been amused by
the effect it produced upon the different birds.
The effect on the whole is decidedly good, for
whereas the larger birds used to get almost all the
bacon, now the small ones get it all, though I
have no doubt the bigger ones take a good deal of
it from them when they fly away, making a cat's
paw of them, as it were. At first when I had
put the plate down they all seemed shy of it.
The little cole tit was the first to venture, and
took a piece off the edge. Then came the tomtit,
very much alarmed but soon reassured, and taking

hold of the edge of the plate with one claw, so as to reach further with its beak. The blue tit is clever with its claws; it holds down a piece of bread with them and picks it to pieces. I see none of the others do that. After this came a robin boldly and jumped straight into the middle of the plate—twice he did this. Then followed the nuthatch, who looked puzzled and afraid, and could not reach any of the bacon, that round the edge having been removed. So I opened the window and put the bacon all on the edge, and when it came again it fed very confidently. Last came the little hedge-sparrow, creeping round the corner as it always does, but it looked much disturbed, and crept back again. All this time several chaffinches had been fluttering about the window, but not one had had courage to come, though their wish to do so was strong, I could see, and they greatly prefer bacon to bread. They are not stupid birds, and perhaps the greater fear of the unknown implies a greater intelligence. I have only seen one chaffinch—a hen—take a piece from the plate, although the other birds, sparrows excepted, are now as much at home with it as I am.

April 15, 1882.

To-day I have peeped into a thrush's nest with young birds in it; yesterday I heard the white-

throat singing vigorously; the day before I saw a
swallow, and a few days before that a chiffchaff
was flitting and chiffchaffing about the roses in
the garden. Three greenfinches also appeared
there this morning, and I have seen a golden-
crested wren about. The nuthatches are the
most constant birds at my window now. If I
come down late I am sure to hear one calling, as
it were, for its breakfast, on the lime-trees opposite.
This morning when I at last opened the window
the bird almost flew in my face. I like to hear
the whirr of its strong wings close to me, though
it reminds me rather of the rapid opening of a fan
by a lady who is a little out of temper.

CHAPTER IV

We have had cold winds lately, and before that strange fogs and mists.

THE FOG

A BALLAD OF DEMOGORGON

'And Demogorgon, a tremendous gloom.'
SHELLEY.—*Prometheus Unbound.*

DEMOGORGON came up the street,
His face was dark and his wings were fleet,
And Demogorgon smelt far from sweet.

Demogorgon grew more and more,
Up he came, and I fled before;
The sea behind did ramp and roar.

I had not time to reach my gate
When Demogorgon came up like fate,
And fell upon me, and swallowed me straight.

He swallowed me up and he swallowed me down,
He swallowed me all with my cloak so brown:
And he swallowed the hills and the sea and the town.

He has left but the bones of the skeleton trees:
He has left me poor painter!—to sneeze and to
    wheeze:
What else can I do without light, if you please,
Unless to make doggerel verses like these?

E

One very misty day I saw upon the sea, near the horizon, a long dark line which might easily have been taken for a sea-serpent, or some long undulating sea beast, for it seemed in continual motion. It did not, however, seem to progress at all; and soon I saw black specks rise from one part of the line and settle down at another part; and I scarcely needed the sudden rising up of two black divers nearer in shore to show me that it was a very large flock of those birds. I never saw a large congregation of them before, but a fisherman to whom I spoke about it did not seem to think it at all wonderful.

April 16, 1882.

A cold wind, and a hungry crowd of birds at the window in consequence. The nuthatch has a wonderful number of notes—cries, rather. I heard a fresh one to-day. I could not have believed that it proceeded from a nuthatch if I had not seen it. The note was more like that of a large mouse; it was a squeak, nothing more nor less, and appeared to be addressed to a companion in the distance; no doubt the note, though not loud, was far-reaching. The bird has become wonderfully tame, and will sometimes feed on the sill as I stand by the open window.

The song of the chaffinch is heard to-day, I think for the first time; I do not mean the chirp,

or piping note. It is incessant when it once
begins, and—to me—is very disagreeable. I have
a friend who dislikes the note of the chiffchaff,
but that can hardly be called a song. I do not
at all dislike its contented little 'chiffchaff,'
though at times it may become rather wearisome ;
but the note of the chaffinch is coarse and harsh.
Besides being plebeian and inharmonious, the
chaffinch is, I think, less useful than the other
birds. I never see it eating the green blight on
the rose-trees, as all the other birds do. Perhaps
it is too heavy to hang on a rose spray; but it
cannot be only that, for the heavy sparrows do a
great deal of good in that way. Perhaps they do
not like it ; but it seems to me that, generally,
birds will eat anything eatable that they can get.

It is curious that the old cock chaffinch, who
is so tame that he flies to the window directly he
sees me there, and begs for a bit of bacon, and
almost takes it out of my hand, is still afraid of
the white plate. I see it sometimes, if it cannot
get anything in any other way, approach it very
shyly, and then dart at a bit and fly away as if it
were red-hot ; it must have had some experience
quite special and peculiar of danger or difficulty
attached to something white. It is by far the
most intelligent bird of all, as well as the most
bold and hungry. Just now it is extremely busy

providing for its young. It comes with its beak full, as one would think, of flies, or perhaps of a large green caterpillar ; but it always manages to take up some of my provision also. It has many a fight with another cock that would like to become my pensioner also, but which is quite cowed by the other. It has brought its young here now and then, but not so constantly as last year. Its nest is in a small juniper just across the lawn ; I can almost see the nest from the window, and could watch the feeding of the young with an opera glass. One of the young flew straight to me from the nest one day, and began to beg for itself.

In another juniper close by——a dead one and therefore just its own colour——my little lame hedge-sparrow built her nest very early, and brought up two young ones, coming to my window for food for them very often, and allowing me to go and put back the bough and look at her or her children without being the least discomposed thereby.

June 10, 1882.

'*Quanto è allegro!*' What bird was it, what happy but heartless little bird that called forth these, the almost last words of Garibaldi? Garibaldi died with the window of his room wide open, while the sun was setting over Corsica. Before

the last agony began, a bird alighted twittering on
his window-sill. Garibaldi saw it, and murmured,
'*Quanto è allegro!*' ('How joyful it is!') Half
child, half hero, he had been all the days of his
wonderful life; it must have been the child in him
that the bird came to greet; and this must have
been the last glad thing that his eyes looked upon.
But the dying man's sufferings were great, and his
words must have sounded half reproachful, and the
song must have jarred painfully on the feelings of
those who were watching the deathbed.

I hope few birds are so heartless, so cruel, as
my old cock chaffinch has proved himself to be in
these last few days—my old chaffinch that has fed
winter after winter at the window, that flies to it
when I open it, and waits till I throw him a bit of
bacon, which he cleverly catches flying, snapping
it up like a dog. As I said in my last note, he
brought his son to learn to feed here (having
reared his young in the juniper opposite), and was
apparently fond and proud of him. But the son
learnt fast, and grew fast, and soon became so
bold and greedy that he pecked at every other
bird that came to the window, even the nuthatch.
That, I suppose, is the reason why the bold bird
came a few days ago in a sadly different and
piteous condition, painfully limping on one weak
leg, tumbling over when a gust of rough wind

met his poor little frame, no longer pecking at
other birds, but shrinking timidly from them.
Apparently he feels most safe close to my window,
where I waste a vast deal of time and useless
sorrow, watching to see that the other birds do
not hurt him, and that he is supplied with crumbs.
He may recover, for he has not lost his foot; I
can see it hanging under the feathers, and he gets
along a little better to-day, and has learnt to make
use of his tail as a support and balance. But he
grows thinner, and his eyes grow less and less
bold and bright. I should not know the bird but
that, when his father comes too, he begins, as well
as his maimed condition will permit, to beg to be
fed. There is that pretty indescribable motion of
the head and wings, that form of entreaty that
the young birds never seem to use except towards
their parents; then for a moment the little thing,
that has suddenly grown so old-looking, looks
young again. And then—alas! that I should have
to say it!—the old bird pecks at it savagely. Not
only does he peck at his child when thus addressed,
but if he hears its cry (which has grown weak and
plaintive, and which can be well distinguished
from the others), he flies up, and begins to peck at
it as if he wished to kill it. The young thing
shrinks away, looks reproachfully, wonderingly, at
its parent, and takes to flight. It is gradually

learning that it is an orphan as well as maimed, and that it is utterly separated from all companionship—except mine. Fortunately it is not much afraid of me; and, with discretion, I can manage to clear the sill of the other birds without frightening it away, though it will look about wonderingly for some time after they have taken flight, and twist its head about with a queer puzzled look, as if it were trying not only to see but to think—to put two and two together, in fact. But I am horrified at that old bird! Does he think his child gets too many crumbs? But I hear the plaintive cry of my little cripple, and I must take my mahlstick and defend it.

June 18, 1882.

Whether it is nature or civilisation that has performed the cure, or both, I cannot say; but I can say with pleasure that the poor little chaffinch has nearly recovered the use of its leg, and that its father seems reconciled to it. But it has not been easy for the maimed bird to get its living, and without my constant crumbs and attention I doubt whether it would have done it. Moreover it has suffered loss. Its ways are feeble and timid, and its colour considerably less brilliant than that of other birds of the same age.

This latter circumstance confirms me in the

notion I have always held that the superior vigour of the male birds and other creatures may well have something to do with their more lively colouring.

June 25, 1882.

I went a little way up the hill to-day, and saw a pretty sight on the way. On the edge of a low roof sat six young swallows (or birds of the swallow kind) all in a row. I am doubtful about the species, because they were so very white: from the front they seemed all white waistcoat except the pretty little mobile heads, and the wings that set up a wonderful quivering and fluttering motion when the parent bird appeared in the distance. For they were being fed. The parent or parents, for I think there were two, were much darker. They were house martins, I think, but they passed so rapidly that I could not be sure. In any case they were devoted parents, and to see all the wings begin to quiver, and the six large mouths to open, and to hear the eager cries, was most interesting. But what pleased me most was the **fraternal** feeling shown among them: only one, or at most two, could receive anything each time the parent visited them; and, as far as I could see, the distribution was anything but impartial. How could the poor birds remember which they had fed last? But though the young things had to wait so much, and to be so often disappointed, there never seemed to be the least anger or irritation in their little white breasts; they bowed without a murmur to the decisions of their parental providence, and not only that, there was unmistakable 'altruism' in the conduct of two of them. These two were one on each side of a third, which seemed weak and unable to keep on its legs; for which reason it had less chance of being fed. At least, so apparently thought one of the others; for it put its beak cleverly and tenderly under the breast of the weak one, and poked and poked till it got it to stand up: then their 'charitable organisation' was evinced, for the two outsiders propped up the feeble one between them, pressing close to it most affectionately. They were chattering all the time busily, but they never relaxed their support even when the dainty and desired bit was presented to one of the three.

The young birds never rose to meet the parent, as White of Selborne describes them as doing; if they had, there would have been a terrible clashing in the air. No; they looked and sounded like a vibrating musical cord as they awaited the parent bird. It had quite the effect of a struck harp-string upon me; not a bird left its place, only stretched itself up as high as it could, and immediately and quietly subsided afterwards.

As for the parent it generally popped the bit
into one of the open mouths as it flew by; sometimes into two; once or twice I saw it catch hold
of the edge of the roof for a moment to steady its
aim at an open mouth. This was not unnecessary,
for I saw one precious morsel dropped 'twixt beak
and beak.

Two or three times the bird flew close to them
without giving anything; had it dropped or
swallowed it? That caused disappointment evidently, there was a general dulling. I watched
till my neck ached, and then went up higher, but
hearing some noisy boys coming up I turned to
look again, and saw that all the little things had
been frightened away except one. Was it the
weak one? The 'solidarité' of the group was
what struck me so much; it was like that of the
long-tailed tits. How different from the selfish
greediness of the young chaffinches!

CHAPTER V

September 19, 1882.

NOTHING worth recording has happened in my little bird-world, since my last entry, or I have been too busy to notice it. The summer has been cold and wet and short; birds abundant, but insect-life less abundant than usual, I think. I think so partly because the birds have been almost as constantly at the window as if it had been winter, and have appeared quite as anxious for a share of the food placed there. Not, however, the tits; of them I have seen but little till now, when they are beginning to come again.

The nuthatches, a beautiful sleek, intelligent pair of birds, with a great deal of character, have become very confident and familiar.

To-day, for the first time, I saw a chiffchaff at my window-sill. It did not take any crumbs though, and had probably been attracted by the sight of a fly. There are numbers of the pretty little things in the garden just now, chasing each other and the flies in the most lively and graceful manner, and so eagerly that they seem to take no notice of me at all. Two of them nearly flew into my face the other day. I was watching them as they flew swiftly in and out among the plants and vegetables in the kitchen garden, and was wondering how they managed to keep so exactly within about a foot of each other, when a sudden turn brought them so directly upon me, and so close, that I involuntarily drew back and shut my mouth lest I should swallow them! Several times they have flown almost as near me; and several times one has flown against the window or fluttered before it, trying to get a fly on the other side.

I conclude that they find it is becoming very difficult to get a living, and that they will soon be gone. I love the little chiffchaffs, and shall be right sorry to lose them.

October 8, 1882.

I have learnt two things lately concerning birds. The first is that rooks know Sundays from week days; and the second is that they are very fond of walnuts.

I fancy that all birds know Sunday; at least I have often been struck when taking a walk during the time of Morning Service—going to rooks' church as it were—with the unmistakable fact that more and rarer birds were to be seen than usual, and that they were more at their ease.

With regard to rooks I am now quite convinced

of it. I have a small walnut tree in my garden.
I planted it myself, and it has not borne fruit more
than two or three years. It stands between my
house and another, and is very near to both. This
year I could see from the window about six or
eight nice little bunches of nuts, and I watched
them with affection. Last Sunday, as I was
sitting writing, I heard a cawing and croaking
close at hand that drew me to the window; and,
behold, there were four or five huge rooks flopping
about upon my poor little tree, trying hard to sit
on its weak branches. I was not sure that they
meant mischief; nevertheless, with some difficulty,
I frightened them away. They came back again,
and again I got rid of them. A third time only
two came back, and then I thought I would watch
and see what happened. In a few moments I saw
one of them fly hastily away, not to the rookery,
but towards the river, with a nice large green
walnut in his beak. Of course I made a very
sensible clatter then, and no more came that day.

This morning, Sunday, I was again unable to
go to church and sat reading, when I heard an
extraordinary noise in the lime-trees opposite the
window, which are far from the rookery. I knew
the noise was made by rooks, but it was not any
of their ordinary cries; it was something between
a scream and a croak. Did it mean 'walnuts,' or

was it the expression of extreme anxiety?—of a
contest between their wish to get the nuts and
their fear of the proximity of the houses? Probably the latter. Whatever it was, down they
came in a few minutes upon my poor little tree,
and I saw one huge creature trying by flapping to
hold on to a top shoot from which he was attempt-
ing to twist a fine green pair of nuts. Great was
the row I made, and I frightened them away. I
did so again. Then I put on my bonnet and went
for a walk up the hill. I was away about an hour
—perhaps rather more. When I came back every
walnut was gone, except one which they could not
reach, and one which they had dropped on the grass.

I have long felt pretty sure that birds take their
pleasure, and enjoy an unwonted freedom of mind
during morning church-time, just as they always
do in the early morning, but I never had a more
striking proof of it than this. For I feel very sure
that no attack was made on my walnuts during
the week; if there had been, I could not have
failed to notice it and to see its effects.

The clusters were but few; they were quite
near the window and I knew each one. I rather
expected to lose them all while I was away, and I
should have gathered them before going out but
that my longest rake would not reach high enough
to shake the bough.

October 15, 1882.

The next Sunday that is, and the rooks came again! Of course they found no walnuts, but one *very* old-looking rook (all rooks look old) would not believe its eyes, but perched upon a branch opposite to the one that had borne most nuts, and began bowing to it—plunging its head forward, and at the same time opening his beak as if he expected a nut to fly into it. After a time the beak, since it took in nothing, gave out each time a sharp, harsh cry. Its gestures were so absurd that I laughed aloud. The rook looked round, but as the window was shut I think it did not see me. It certainly had a good memory, for it knew exactly where the largest group of walnuts had been. Why then could it not remember that they had been taken?

October 22, 1882.

No rooks came to-day, but they have been floating about overhead, evidently speculating on the subject of walnuts.

On the other hand there has been—added to the showers of hail and rain and golden leaves—quite a shower, as one may say, of tits at the window. They are coming back, I suppose, from their country quarters. One called my attention to the fact, a few days ago, by flying twice against the window, striking it with wings and beak. I

went to see what was the matter, and there it
stood—an old bird, I think an *habitué*—in a fluff
of indignation, between a sparrow and a chaffinch.
Did it wish to call me to its assistance in the
maintenance of its rights, or was it trying to fly
through the window, just a little bit afraid of the
two strong beaks?

November 12, 1882.

I saw to-day, for the first time since the very
hard winter that slew so many birds, a long-tailed
tit. It was very shy. There was a golden-crested
wren in the garden the other day. My attention
was called to it by the scolding of a small blue tit,
who chose to consider it an intruder. The birds
are already very tame at my window; quite a
little flock of them come to greet me. I do not
mean that they all settle upon the window-sill
together. They are far too much afraid of each
other for that. But they come and go and flit
about till I put out the food, and then they take a
bit and a snap, or stay and feed, as the case may
be.

I believe I have as my pensioners one pair of
nuthatches (one is smaller than the other, and I
suppose it is a pair; but they never come quite
together, and seem very much afraid of one
another), four blue tits, two cole tits, one robin
(or two, I am not sure; there are two about, a

pair I suppose, but they are more timid than any
other bird), three or four chaffinches, one hedge-
sparrow, and any number of house-sparrows.
Very distinct characters, all of them. The
chaffinches I can now distinguish from one
another. One I call Flick, one Schmuck, but the
old one who comes most constantly and flies to
catch what I throw to him I call Old Joe. He is
cross and covetous, and I think he overfeeds
himself and is getting gouty; he hops with
great difficulty. To-day, however, I interrupted
a stand-up fight between him and one of the
nuthatches. Few birds will challenge a nuthatch.
I saw a blue tit do so the other day; but then the
nuthatch had a bit of bacon in his beak, which
rather diminished the power of that dreaded
weapon. The cole tits, one of which is much
smaller than the other, always wait till the nuthatch has filled his beak and left; then they are
down upon the plate in a minute. They do not
seem to care for crumbs; all the birds prefer
bacon. Old Joe refuses bread till he is sure he
can get no bacon.

A robin in the midst of three or four tits
makes a pretty bit of colour. Sometimes I have
a *wreath* of tits before the window; for a light
branch of the Gloire de Dijon rose springs like an
arch from the edge of the verandah, and the tits

F

generally alight there first, to see if all is safe. A rose looked up from below just in the middle of it a short time ago. There is an abundance of buds upon the tree still, but I suppose they will not now come to anything.

When the wind and rain cease for a day the weather is cold and frosty. A more unpleasant autumn I do not remember. A few roses still manage to open. They look like jewels in the midst of the green lawn; but the trees are almost bare, and the leaves, instead of lying like gold beneath them, are sodden and beaten into the ground.

AUTUMN

'Paga tuí ; tuí lieta un dì.'
Il Ratto di Proserpina.

Upon a fallen tree by storms laid low,
Amid the harvest-fields, despoiled and bare,
Sad Autumn sits. The sunset from her hair
Fades slowly; slowly fades the flush and glow
Of ruddy splendour from the bramble-crown
Above her brows; and one by one fall down
The gold leaves, crimson-splashed. About her knees
The tattered purple clings, and harsh and sere
The stubble 'neath her feet; while in her ear
The fateful voice of Winter, heard afar,
Yet ever nearer, seems to pierce and freeze
Her shuddering life-blood, and the beauty mar
Of form and feature; while the darkening air
Grows still and thick with horror and despair.

Anon a tempest rises in her soul,
And flashes fires of anguish from her eyes,
While round about the angry thunders roll,
And groans and shrieks assail the heedless skies;
But soon the passionate fire falls down and dies.

Then sinks the queenly head upon her hands——
A broken flower; then loosed are sorrow's bands;
Like winds in leafless tree-tops come her sighs,
Like flooded streams her tears; till, worn with woe,
She thinks no more upon her golden gain
Reft from her—of her glory all laid low;
Her vines and orchards stript, her flowers dead;
But watches as the frost-breath o'er the plain
Steals slowly; draws her mantle o'er her head,
And waits the cold inevitable chain.

So much for Autumn. But what do the dying leaves say who 'leave their buds behind'? That makes a difference. This is their farewell:

SONG OF THE DYING LEAVES

'FAREWELL!' the brown leaves sigh,
 'Farewell! we needs must go!'
Trembling they fly, then fall and die,
 Sighing and murmuring low.

'Farewell, O summer breeze,
 Playmate of golden hours!
Seek us no more on the tall swaying trees,
 But with the dying flowers.

' Gaily we danced and played
   All the long summer day ;
Sweet was thy breath o'er thyme-buds thou
      hadst strayed ;
   Feed now on our decay.

' Birds, though so blithe ye be,
   Farewell ye too must say :
But while we flee to our mouldy death-bed, ye
   O'er sunny seas flit away.

' Do not forget our sighs,
   Pleasant our shade has been
Pleasant the gleam of your soft brown eyes,
   Peeping the boughs between.

' Birds, blithesome birds, farewell !
   Still let the robin's note,
Chanting our requiem and ringing our knell,
   Over our low grave float.

' Children, and lovers true,
   Friends who beneath us strayed,
Watching the gold lights glittering through,
   Do not forget our shade.

' We leave our buds behind,
   Each in its perfect place ;
Folded and firm, its brown robe warmly lined,
   Waiting the world to grace.

' Let not the worm intrude,
   Nor tooth of frost so keen ;
O World ! O Winds ! your ways are rough and
      rude,
   Touch not their tender green !

' And when their broadening shade
  Covers the green-sward hot,
There, where we once our sheltering shadows
    laid,
  O World, forget us not !

' Farewell ! we needs must go !
  Farewell ! ' the brown leaves sigh,
Trembling they go ; sighing and murmuring low,
  Gently they fall and die.

CHAPTER VI

1883

THE year begins wet and warm as the last did. The thrush sings in the dawn of the morning almost as if it were February, and I have heard the note of the greater titmouse.

The birds at the window are in an extraordinary state of friskiness and flightiness. There has been a third cole tit of late; very small and thin and much afraid of the others. They did their best from the first to chase it away; but it comes still, and is not now afraid of the bacon, as it was at first.

The cole tits take away a large part of the bacon; it is impossible that they can eat it all, and so speedily. I suppose the other birds get it from them. They have no fear of me at all through the window, and come fluttering down directly I make my appearance in the morning. One drops down into the middle of the plate without even the ceremony of looking to see if I am there or not, and carries off great bits, or packets

of bits, of bacon. That one never stays to eat,
and evidently carries for others. I hope the
robin gets some of it ; he comes so seldom himself.

January 4, 1883.

He came, however, this morning, when no
other bird would do so. I went to the window
with a scarlet woollen wrap over my head, as I
had a cold. All the birds were frightened at me,
dreadfully frightened, except the robin. He looked
up at me for a few minutes, very earnestly, from
the verandah, sang a little song, and then flew up
and fed close to me. This he did twice. Did he
think I was another sort of robin? or was it the
attraction of protective colouring? The latter
probably. I know robins feel the protection of a
brown dress. That sense of protective colour is,
I suppose, one of the most primitive.

February 8, 1883.

I must not allow Old Joe, the old chaffinch, to
pass away without a note. He made his last
appearance without a tail : he looked very much
ashamed of himself, and as if he would have put
it between his legs if he had had one ; but then
he would not have been ashamed, not he ! And
it may have been the tail-between-legs look that I
took for shame. But the birds were disgusted,

and pecked at him, poor fellow; and he dropped
himself down off the verandah, and has never
appeared again. I had noticed for some time past
that he walked in a slow and gouty manner, and
looked old. Probably a cat, from which he was
too slow to escape, drew the feathers out in trying
to catch him; or it may have been the anger of
other birds, for I must confess that Joe had been
latterly behaving very badly to them. He kept
watch over the plate of food even when he could
eat no more himself, and pecked at every bird
that came near—even the nuthatch. I cannot,
therefore, but feel—having, for a woman, a rather
quick sense of justice—that Old Joe probably
brought his fate upon himself. But I miss him;
he used to fly to the window directly I appeared
in the morning, and was not content till I had
myself thrown him a morsel, which he generally
caught in his beak. He then used to retire under
a rose-branch—a secluded corner where he could
not be pounced upon—to eat it.

Another chaffinch seems disposed to fill his
place, but is not yet quite so confident of my
benevolent feelings towards him, though I have
no doubt he is one of the two or three broods that
Old Joe taught to feed on my window-sill.

A pair of nuthatches have become very tame;
they look me straight in the face when my head,

PIED WOODPECKERS

spectacles and all, is close to them, and seem quite
to demand food when there is none.

Some of the blue tits are equally tame now,
and the robin is a little bolder ; but the cole tits
seem to become rather wilder, and I dare say I
shall soon lose them. I had five little blue tits all
together one day ; so fat and funny, so pugnacious
and greedy they were ! I believe I like them the
best of all my birds, and I am sure they have more
intelligence than the others. I wonder whether
their brain is comparatively larger. The head of
the cole tit looks far larger in comparison with the
rest of the body, and they seem intelligent too.
Till this winter, however, they have not been here
so much as the blue tits, and I have therefore had
less opportunity of learning their ways at the
window.

March 16, 1884.

A whole year has passed since I last made a
note in this book. To-day two things occurred
that ought to be noticed. I have seen a pair of
spotted woodpeckers—a bird I believe I never saw
before ; and I have heard an owl hoot and another
answer it in the daytime—a thing I certainly never
heard before. It was curious to watch the spotted
woodpecker ; it was too high above me, but I
could see the vibration of the tail that accompanied
the whirring noise that it made in boring a hole

in an old branch of a tree. It reminded me of a
bee trying to sting through a thick glove.

These notes were brought to a pause by a long
and severe illness last year, and it is pleasant
to record the fact that when, after six weeks' seclu-
sion upstairs, I came again to the drawing-room
window, I was immediately greeted by one of the
little blue tits. It first fluttered before the window,
and then, settling on the sill close to me, began
bowing and scraping and lowering its wings in
the prettiest way imaginable. It could not have
expressed its welcome (and no doubt its wish to
be fed) more eloquently if it had had words at its
command.

The birds soon came back to me, and I fed
them all the summer. Some young robins became
very tame, though they did not come much to this
window; they would feed out of my hand in the
garden, and sit up close to me whilst I picked
peas, and even settled on the pot into which I
was putting cuttings. The painting of the house
eventually scared them away; but at one time
they used to come into the room constantly, and
would sit on a book before me as I wrote at the
table. The tamest of them would fly to my hand
for crumbs, and had a splendid scarlet breast
before it became wild.

In January of this year a very tame robin

began to come to the window, and was very bold, sending all the other birds ' to the right about ' ; coming when called, even from the other end of the lawn, and sitting by me with the greatest confidence as I worked by the window. But I am afraid it was an old robin that felt its end approaching, and came for a little assistance ; for one day it had a dreadful fit before my eyes,

NUTHATCHES

and fell down on the lawn below. I ran down, expecting to see it dead ; it was still in convulsions, but slowly recovered, and seemed pretty well next day. After that it appeared no more, and when I was told that a dead robin had been picked up in the shrubbery opposite to the window, I felt sure it was my little friend.

Nuthatches abound this year, and are full of confidence, but afraid of each other. One is very large and finely coloured, and I can easily distinguish it from the others. The smaller ones are very much afraid of it; and if by an unlucky chance one of them alights near the plate at the same moment as the larger one, a very curious little performance is to be observed. The smaller one stands a little on one side, and avoids—carefully and fearfully avoids—looking at the other. It dares not fly away (this I have observed with other birds too) lest its enemy should fly after it; so it pretends not to see, hoping, therefore, not to be seen; or possibly it is merely that the hen waits till her mate has fed, before beginning herself. The hedge-sparrow also acts strangely on a similar occasion. It is a larger bird than most of my visitors, and the tits are often afraid of it; but it has a very small beak and head, and I observe that it endeavours, while keeping an eye on the nuthatch and its beak towards it (its lance in rest, i.e.) to hide its head under its ample feathers. I have observed these performances so many times that I feel quite sure of their meaning. The small cole tit has a comparatively large head, and accordingly its wits are its defence. It seizes the moment when the nuthatch has flown off with a beak full of bacon, and slips quietly and confidently into the plate, quite sure that the larger bird will not be back immediately. When two nuthatches

are feeding the case is more difficult and complex
for the little thing, and it will wait on the bough
close by, sometimes for four or five minutes, till it
feels sure that the coast is clear. The sparrows
treat the little birds so badly, that I do not mind
sending them away. The nuthatches I cannot
help liking too much for that; they are such queer
picturesque birds, with so much frank character.
I feel sure some of them know me: they ought to
do so by the way they stare me full in the face,
and I often think one is shouting at me from a tree
when I walk out into the garden. I believe that
the blue tits greet me also.

March 28, 1884.

In spite of the blackthorn winter the birds go
on building with vigour; and I was much
interested to-day by what I saw in the tree
opposite my window. I believe it was a lesson in
building, or rather in the fetching of materials,
given by an old rook to a young one. A large
lumbering creature had been there previously, and
had been working with much deliberation and reflection. It evidently expended much intelligence
in the choice of its twigs, and much dexterity and
strength in carrying them away. Then came two
other rooks; one began to work away with great
rapidity and eagerness, and at the same time—as
it seemed to me—with a great deal of conscious

pride in its ability; it seemed aware that the other
rook was looking on, as indeed it did, with great
interest, but without taking any part in the labour.
'That must be the lady,' thought I, remembering
how, when two goldfinches built a nest close to
my window and I watched the proceedings, one
bird only fetched the materials, while the other
sat on the rail or worked at the nest. But no;
this was a different case. When the worker had
as many twigs as it could carry, it flew away; but
the looker-on, instead of following, as I expected,
flew down after a few moments of reflection to the
place where the first had worked, and began to
try to do the same. It did not succeed in getting
off a single twig. though it tried hard, and at last
it flew away—to take another lesson perhaps. I
have seen birds teach their young to feed on my
window-sill, and I have heard a singing lesson
given by an old robin to a young one more than
once. Of this I feel sure; for after every stave
the smaller voice tried hard to repeat it, and the
old one listened so intently that it was not easy to
disturb it; so I do not doubt that 'twigging'
also is taught to birds. They inherit a great deal,
but not everything; and perhaps, as with ourselves,
what they inherit has to be cultivated.

March 30, 1884.

A canary came to the verandah to-day. I opened the window a little, and it flew up and seemed about to come in, and then——struck by some strangeness, I suppose——flew away. A few minutes afterwards it was beating itself against the window of the landing, and trying to get in. I opened the window an inch and spoke to it, and it chirped and shook its wings, but when I opened the window more, away it flew again. Again I saw it at the window, and I heard that it had come about the kitchen door with the other birds. Whilst I was looking for it out of the hall window, I suddenly perceived two dark brown eyes close to me, looking earnestly at me from the midst of the clematis. A blackbird has built a nest there, and is sitting apparently. I can see it as I go up and down the steps to the door. I hope no one else will do so, but alas! it is dreadfully exposed, and if the clematis does not make haste and come into leaf and hide it, the next boy that passes will certainly see it. The old thrush's nest still remains there, though it was built several years ago; and as the thrush brought up at least one family there, I hope the blackbird may do so.

June 13, 1884.

But it did *not*. It sat for some time there; but one day I heard a loud outcry—such as only

G

an alarmed blackbird can make—and the nest was abandoned. I could not reach it to look into it, but I conclude that a crow stole the eggs. A pair of chaffinches, who built in the same clematis, probably for the sake of being near my provision on the window-sill, were more fortunate, and brought up three little ones, who all came tumbling out of the nest one day, very prematurely, frightened by my inadvertently moving the clematis with a rake. Two lodged in the branches and got back again; the other I had to pick up and put back. It had two little fluffy feathers, like ears, standing up over its eyes.

The young birds have been very amusing this year, and very abundant. As for the sparrows, there must be scores about in the garden, and they keep down the green blight most delightfully. Let no one say—as I believe Miss Ormerod does—that sparrows will not eat them. I watch them constantly devouring the aphides as fast as they can. The old ones do a good deal; but the young ones, being lighter, can rest on smaller sprays. Young sparrows seem to be more voracious than any other birds; they follow their mothers about till they, poor things, seem fairly puzzled where to get food for so many. The swallowing seems to be the difficulty, in which assistance is required from the mother; even when they have plenty of crumbs before them, and can peck them up, they still stand shaking their wings and begging to be fed.

I was very much amused the other day; I heard an infantine cry at the window, and going there, found a young nuthatch asking a tom-tit to feed it. It was funny to see the eagerness of the large helpless baby, and the indignant astonishment, not unmixed with alarm, of the little tit. It was an old blue tit, and accustomed to fly before the beak of the nuthatch, but quite at home with me. And there it stood with one claw in the plate, staring first at me and then at the nuthatch, which opened its great beak and shook its wings in the most childish manner, until at last, tired of waiting, it flew away.

A flight of long-tailed tits passed through the garden yesterday. They were gone in no time; like a flight of arrows they came from the limes to the sycamore. One stayed just to feed a young one, and then away again. I enjoyed the passing sight of them though: directly I hear that well-known fluting, of which I heard so much last spring, I am on the *qui vive*. But they will never stay here now that houses and gardens have taken the place of orchards.

Some birds seem to appreciate more highly than others the comparative shelter that a garden

affords. May we not also fancy that they may like
the flowers? They seem to choose their homes
and build their nests with an eye to beauty. A
quite lovely nest a pair of robins have built this
year in the pendent ivy by the side of the tool
shed; and in it, though in such an exposed place,
they have managed to rear three young ones.
Dear little things, I was so glad of them! One
day I found the nest empty and the parents in a
terrible state of mind. Two of their children
were about in the garden, but were so very small
and badly clothed that I came to the conclusion
a cat had frightened them out of their nest too
soon, and had perhaps taken the third. The
parent robins have been in such an ungovernable
rage ever since, whenever a cat has made its appearance, that I feel sure there must have been
some unusual cause of offence. I have seen them
sit both together on a rose-branch that overhangs
the wall, and shriek at the cat like mad things,
flapping their wings at her as if they thought they
could frighten her away. I could hardly help
laughing, though their agony was most tragically
real. The young birds are grown to a safer size
now, and can fly away. One fluttered in at the
kitchen window lately. It was caught, and I put
it back behind the faggots where the old robin
tried hard to keep them.

I suppose few birds have so many different notes as the robin, or such expressive ones. The warning note, and the angry note, all must have observed ; but I am not so sure that the long, pathetic, soft note, which is, I think, meant to draw the young ones into shelter and away from some danger, has been noticed. I have heard the note often this year, and believe that to be the motive.

A blackbird must have had its nest near. It carried away the best part of the bacon in my plate for about a fortnight, and then brought a pair of fine young ones to feed on the lawn, and even on the window-sill sometimes. There is no note I love better than the blackbird's, so I was quite content to feed them.

A greenfinch built in an *arbor-vitæ*, but found the nest too exposed and did not lay any eggs in it. A hedge-sparrow, I think, reared its young behind some sticks, and a wren in the shed. The robin has laid five eggs again in its pretty nest ; but I never see it sitting on them : it is now so very much exposed, and I am so much in the garden, that I do not expect it will have the courage to do so, which is a pity.

The garden looks lovely. The rose-trees are covered with beautiful blooms and buds, and with splendid foliage. Against the background of lime-trees stands out in one angle of the house a group composed of Oriental poppies and tall blue Florentine irises, mixed with yellow day-lilies, and overhung with large white clematis. The birds must love the flowers I feel sure.

KEEP and hold in a crimson fold,
　　Rose, thy passionate sweetness;
Let the brown bee dip, and the butterfly sip,
But keep it safe from the sun's hot lip
　　And dark Death's fiery fleetness.
Yet come he will, and come he may,
For if we thought that no decay
　　Would follow thy completeness,
Should we love thee, Rose — ah, who can say?
Should we love thee then as we do to-day,
　　With thy perishing passionate sweetness?

CHAPTER VII

September 9, 1884.

FLOCKS of chiffchaffs in the garden for two or three days, to the great annoyance of the robins and the great amusement of J. M. H. The pretty little, graceful, playful things seem to pay no attention to anything but the insects and each other : they have a delight in motion evidently. I saw one balancing itself on the overarching top of a stalk of maize, and I wondered how much it might weigh.

Yesterday I went down to the river to sketch, and saw four or five of those lovely grey wagtails, darting from point to point, or flickering over the pools like magnificent butterflies. Some seemed less brilliantly yellow beneath : were they young, or females?

One little robin still haunts the nest in the ivy. It seems of a retiring disposition, but is very sociable. It almost always comes out from under the asparagus or some other covert when I begin to garden, and sits close to me, gurgling a little low song in its throat, so soft you can hardly hear

it, and looking up to me with one eye in the most
insinuating manner. It has never yet been driven
away from me by an old robin, as so often happens ;
but I have seen it listen and then fly away on
hearing one in the distance.

December 1, 1884.

Is it quite as certain as Mr. Romanes appears
to think, that the bark of the dog, and its talent
for watching and caretaking, are derived from
human companionship? I think he would doubt
it if he could see the very pugnacious robin that
now sits almost continually on the edge of my
verandah (after having fed moderately from my
plate), watching for the other birds, and flying at
them when they come near the food. Its action
is wonderfully dog-like as it stands there with its
head down, flapping its wings and making little
half-leaps which are accompanied by short sharp
notes that have all the characters of a bark, and
appear to have the same cause and the same effect.
For my part I think it is the other way, and that
it is part of our animal and not of our distinctively
human nature, that snaps and barks, and watches
over its property and seeks to get everything for
itself. I never saw so pugnacious a robin as this
is ; he drives away even the stout old chaffinch
that has been ' cock of the walk ' for years. He is
down on the other birds so suddenly that they

have not time to think whether or not he is really
a very powerful adversary. He never, however,
flies at the tits. Perhaps they are beneath his
notice; or perhaps he thinks they cannot eat
much. I have seen even him fly before the
nuthatch: this, however, he does not always do,
though I doubt whether he would dare *attack* one,
unless its beak was pre-occupied with bacon. I
say 'he' because of the bird's militant character,
but I have no idea whether it is a cock or hen.
It is a curiously short, thick bird, with fierce eyes
—watchful and intelligent.

What a wonderful ear the thrush must have!
I saw one on the lawn a little while ago, listening,
as they do, for worms, close to a noisy lawn-mower
that was being worked in the next garden. It
appeared to have no difficulty in finding the
worms by its ear as usual! I saw something not
so wonderful, but much more distressing, on that
lawn a short time ago—a blackbird pecking out
the eyes of another blackbird! I had seen them
sparring some time before, and did not disturb
them. I wish now that I had done so, for on
going to the window a few minutes later, one bird
was struggling on the ground, the other over it,
and pecking hard at its eyes. I rushed down, but
they were gone. I shall never again listen with
so much pleasure to the singing of a blackbird.

December 25, 1884.

A tom-tit in his war-paint, bristling and
bouncing, is apparently a terrific object to other
birds ; he is certainly a very comical one. Even
more comical is my pugnacious robin. He keeps
up that character, and continues to sit, day by day,
on the edge of the verandah, as round as a ball (he
is very short-winged), looking about for something

TOM-TIT

to fight with, and putting himself into the most
ridiculous attitudes, alternately inquisitive and
defiant. He has, however, become much more
tame ; he comes to the window directly I make
my appearance in the morning, and flies up to
receive his little bit of bacon. But he will not
take it from my hand ; he seems afraid of that. I
argue thence that it is an old robin, as young
robins soon become accustomed to the hand.

January 25, 1885.

A piebald sparrow made its appearance here one day lately; a great contrast to the others, some of which are unusually black about the head. It perched on the verandah whilst the robin was sitting there. The robin gave a start and a jump; without doubt it recognised the strangeness of the sparrow's apparel. It looked up at me as if to see what I thought of it; then again at the sparrow, and then flew down to the lawn below.

Two robins are constantly here now, and have become more friendly; indeed it is easy to see that they are already ' making up to each other.' They have been doing the strangest thing to-day ! Fascination is no doubt the object; but to human eyes their usual demeanour is much more fascinating. I heard a queer little rapid song going on, and went to the window; and there were my two robins standing face to face on the edge of the verandah, and going through a wonderful and ludicrous performance. First one and then the other kept up a kind of dance and song, attitudinising like ballet dancers or nautch girls. One very pleasing attitude appeared to be throwing the head forward and on one side, and gazing fervently at the sky. Whilst one of them acted the other looked on in a state of admiring stupefaction. They were not easily disturbed or my laughter would have discomposed them. At another time I saw one robin taking lively leaps of a foot or two into the air, apparently without the aid of its wings. Another little trick transfigured the bird so completely that I could not believe it to be the same till it came up to the window afterwards—quite its old self. It had managed to make itself very small and upright, with a high crest and a prominent beard, which went on wagging about as the little thing warbled very softly and rapidly, with wild eyes directed towards the other robin.

The blue tit that took up arms against the others has appeared again of late in such a tiger-like and malicious state of mind that I am obliged to chase it away. How does the creature do it? It frightens them all—even the nuthatch, with whom it had a pitched battle lately. It suddenly seems made of steel, and looks as sharp as a spear-head; then it crouches like a tiger, and spreads its wings and rushes—and away goes any bird whatever, even my bold robin. When I frighten it away from the window-sill it attacks the birds that settle on the roses near. The bird must be possessed by a devil of some kind. The very expression of its face is savage, and its attitudes are still more so. It moves its head in a wiry, snake-like way that I never saw in a bird before.

There is a quite wonderful difference in the character of individual birds even of the same kind. The large-headed birds certainly seem to me the most intelligent. The little cole tit, for instance, seems more than half head, and it is curious to see how its quickness and ingenuity serve it in the place of size and strength. One little thing I generally find waiting here in the morning for its bacon. It flies towards the window and flutters a greeting in my face, but then looks about for the robin, knowing well that I always wait till he is there, and then open the window and feed him first.

I had a strange experience one frosty night lately. I was just going off to sleep when there came a lovely note from the window—soft and penetrating and single. I started up and listened, quite bewildered. After a pause it came again, and this time not single but combined with others that left no doubt that it was an owl sitting on the sill. But it was the mellowest, downiest song ever heard. It came again and again, and I was quite sorry when it left. I heard it again further off, and then it was more owlish. I suppose it softened its note when so near the house out of precaution lest it should wake the inmates.

TAWNY OWL

OWL SONG

To-night I heard an Owl call, out of an old elm-tree:
'Hulhúllalalóo!' it seemed to say, and I thought it
  called to me.

'Now, Owl, I pray, what do you say, alone in the dark
  on the tree?'
'O nó-no-no-nó!' the Owl replied; 'it is not dark to me!'
'Then, Owl, tell me, what do you see?' 'Blind mice,
  one, two, and three:
'Hullúllalalóo! to my mate I call, to come and sup
  with me.'

April 2, 1885.

There have been young robins about for two
or more months. Is it my feeding them, or the
mildness of the winter, that has made them so
early? They are almost fully red-breasted, and
already quite tame—to me, at least—coming when
I call them if they are near enough to see me.
The old ones make a rendezvous of my window,
and stand here listening for the voices of their
young ones—listening very anxiously apparently
sometimes, too anxiously to eat; sometimes waiting with a bit in the beak till they have heard the
right song, and then away goes the bird and the
bit. I think there are two broods about, some
younger than the others. I have heard the soft,
long, calling note of the mother more than once.
I say mother instead of parent; but I do not know,
only guess, that it is the mother that makes that
pathetic appeal.

May 25, 1885.

Thrushes about this year, but not blackbirds.
Perhaps they are offended or inconvenienced by

the constant imitation of their note by the starlings.

I think my little cole tits (one little pair has been very constant and tame all the spring) are only just building their nest. One came yesterday with a beakful of sycamore blossoms; it was passing, apparently, but turned aside on seeing my plate of bacon. The little thing was about to peck at the bacon when it seemed to remember that its beak was already filled, and flew away busily in the direction of an orchard near, which I have no doubt is full of birds this year, as the house is unoccupied. The cole tits have such pretty, dainty ways that I should think their nests ought to be very delicate affairs. I had a goldcrest about my *arbor-vitæ* lately, but I think the other birds objected to its presence.

My two tame robins are almost worn out with the labour and anxiety of bringing up their family. Two little things were cheeping about in the garden a few days ago, but I think they have gone further now. One was picked up by my servant at the gate some time ago, and brought in for the night. Workmen have been painting and plastering the house outside, which has increased the trouble of the parent birds; but, on the other hand, there are no cats next door this year. Very thin and shabby my poor little robins

look now. The cock has lost the courage that
made it attack other birds, but it now and then,
when the men are away, sits in its old place on
the verandah. It comes at my call, even from
the trees sometimes, and seems glad of its bacon,
though it will not be drawn aside by it from that
continual listening, listening for the little dull and
distant chirp, or *cheep*, of the young birds. That
sound is called 'weeping' here in Devonshire, I
find; in the Bible it was 'peeping' in the account
of Hezekiah's illness. The Revisers have, I see,
altered it to 'chirping.' I should call it 'cheeping.' Probably when we pronounced the *i* in the
Continental manner, peep was spelt 'pipe.'

June 20, 1885.

I thought I had lost my robin. Only one has
come of late, I think, and this one did not seem
to like the new and much lighter colour of the
verandah, probably thinking it was now too much
exposed. I breakfast downstairs, too, in the
dining-room now. On the sill of that window,
however, he appeared a few days ago, just as I
was thinking I had lost him. I was at breakfast,
and called him and threw some crumbs on the
carpet, and he came in and took some, but
seemed afraid to stay. He has come at my call
twice lately. To-day, when I went to the window

at dinner-time, he flew up close to me and was glad of some crumbs, but, as he was eating them, one of its two young ones came hopping up to share the food. Immediately the old one flew at it and drove it away, and it did not return. And no doubt the reason why the old one so seldom comes now is that it would be setting a bad example to the young ones, who have to be taught to fear human treachery. The old ones are right, no doubt, but I am sorry.

June 22, 1885.

The garden is full of young birds; to-day a family of blackcaps took possession of it for a little while. I saw them here a short time ago when they were younger, but I never had a visit from blackcaps *en famille* before. They were very shy.

Yesterday the garden was indeed *possessed*. I never saw anything like it. I think the birds knew that it was Sunday, and that there would be no shopboys or other comers. A hen blackbird brought three of her children—such a noisy crew—and dug a large hole for them in my central rose-bed. She pecked and scratched and flung the earth about just as a mother hen does for her chicks, and the young blackbirds pecked away at what she turned up just as young chickens do. Only it was all done with much more noise and violence; one would have thought the old bird wanted to dig up a rose-tree. It was an amusing sight, and she must have gone on with her excavations for a quarter of an hour or more. I saw young thrushes being fed too. There were sparrows and chaffinches innumerable, also robins and a water-wagtail. I think that now the roses are coming out, the insects form a great attraction to the birds. If Miss Ormerod could see the way in which the young sparrows pounce down upon the rose-trees here, and strip them of blight, she would no longer doubt that they eat it. Eat it when they can get it, that is; but when they are older and heavier it is not so easy. A sparrow cannot hang on the point of a leaf or sit on a bud as a tit does; but where sparrows can rest, there they will feed greedily on the aphides. I think, to judge by the way in which they tumble about, they have to learn by experience what will support them.

July 1, 1885.

The birds that I supposed were blackcaps may have been marsh tits. I had a young marsh tit yesterday on the roses close at hand, making the same complaining little note. The black head deceived me.

My robin is in and out of the window continually, feeding on the bacon scraps that I place

in the corner of the room for him, or on my desk.
He is not the least afraid, but seems to think it is
a secret between us, and so he never comes in if
another bird is near. He carries away a good
deal, and has, I think, young ones below. If so,
that must be a third brood.

I have the very noisiest little wren in the
garden this year that I ever knew; and I think it
is the smallest, although, from its ways and general
appearance, it seems to be an old one. I do not
know what I had done to offend it yesterday; but
it sat down in the path before me with tail and
beak well up in the air, and scolded at me as if I
had been robbing its nest; the little thing was in
a perfect passion. Perhaps it did not expect me
to be gardening just then, and was building a nest
in the faggots close by. It built one first so very
near a door and path where there was much going
to and fro that I think it was obliged to abandon
it. This is in a fuchsia-tree, and looks very
pretty, but is very conspicuous. I put my finger
in one day when I thought it was abandoned, and
found it cold and empty. I put it in later, and
there was one minute egg; again I tried, and the
egg was gone—removed to another nest, I fancy.

July 6, 1885.

The abundance of young birds about just now
is wonderful; quite unusual, I think. They over-

flow from the garden into the house. I was going
to water a large pot of Agapanthus in the hall this
evening, and had indeed begun doing so, when I
saw a young robin sitting there and looking at me.
I must have wetted the little feet. It seemed all
mouth and fluff about the head; but when I had
caught it (which I was obliged to do, as it flew upstairs), and taken it out of doors, it flew easily to
the nearest tree. A young thrush was also caught
on the top of a picture this morning; and yesterday I had to catch a garden-warbler and to put it
out, lest it should pound itself to death against the
window. Earlier in the year I had to catch a
nuthatch, which wanted to bite.

I put my robin's food in the room now, having
discovered that he knew where to find it and
would come for it. This saves the trouble of
driving off sparrows and chaffinches (no others
come now), and it is pleasant to have the little
fellow hopping in and out so confidently and continually. He takes away a good deal for his young
ones. He still looks on his visits as our secret;
he comes in so quietly, and will not come at all if
another bird is near.

July 28, 1885.

The robin came in twice yesterday, and flew
about the room in an excited and inquiring
manner. He began by flying towards me on the

sofa, and made a circuit nearly round my head.
I felt flattered, and thought it was a mark of
affection from my little friend.   But the second
time another person was on the sofa; and I am
inclined to think that the attraction was a tall
figure of Dante's Beatrice hanging over the sofa.
She is clothed in a long flowing garment of bright
scarlet over a white tunic, and stands against a
bright sky.   From the colouring, the picture is as
likely to attract a robin as it once did a little boy
of about three years old, who was sitting to me
for his portrait.   ' That's a nice girl,' he remarked,
peeping round me and my easel.   The robin loves
scarlet, I suppose, or he would not be scarlet; and
I judge so too from the way in which he now and
then looks down at his own waistcoat.

November 15, 1885.

I doubt whether it is this same robin (more
likely it is one of its children) that now feeds at
my window, and has done so for more than a
month.   His ways are different; or hers——I think
it is a hen, from its want of boldness towards other
birds, and from the delicate, almost whispered,
song that it sings to me now and then.   It calls
me to the window with a peculiar sharp little
chirp that I do not think it uses on other occasions.
I hear it at once; and if I do not go at once to

the window, the bird repeats it more loudly, and again and again till I appear. But it seems to wish not to be heard by the other birds, more especially by a certain pert hen chaffinch that waits for the crumbs that fall from the robin's table, and that does not always wait, but that flies upon the prey as I fling it down to the privileged little thing sitting with its back to me on the edge of the verandah, looking over its shoulder, and greeting me with a gratified flap of its wings when I appear. That, I suppose, I am to take for a smile. It does not often come up thence to feed, as I do not put the plate out yet. I leave it on my desk near the open window when I go out of the room, and it comes in and feeds at its leisure. Last Sunday it came in, I do not know by what window or door (probably the front door, which was invitingly open), and regularly explored the house. I do not think there was more than one room that it did not visit, and of that the door was closed. I followed, to let it out, but it did not care for me, or avail itself of the window I opened. Now, however, windows must be closed, and we (i.e. I and the birds) must return to winter ways, for there was a first white frost this morning.

This morning the tits and nuthatches made their appearance again at breakfast; very smart

and cheery, but as tame as ever. Birds have a
good memory for some things. I think my little
robin really loves me and feels grateful ; it sits on
a rose-spray that has crept under the verandah,
and looks down on me while I dine in the room
below ; I think it is its night-roost. It sings
gently to me all the time ; or rather it makes
significant listening pauses ; and perhaps after all
it is singing to an answering mate, and not to me
at all ! At any rate, it looks quite bewitching
there, pressing its little soft red and white bosom
against its green perch, and warbling most delightfully.

November 28, 1885.

Do herons eat little birds ? Surely not ; yet I
think it was a heron that to-day filled the red
breast of Bob with mortal alarm. At least so it
seemed. I heard him piping on the edge of the
verandah as usual, asking for a bit of bacon ; but
when I went to the window, opened it and threw
the bacon to him, instead of picking it up, he stood
quite still, with his right eye laboriously turned
towards the zenith ; and so he remained, staring.
I called to the bird, asked what was the matter,
threw more bacon ; but he did not move. Then I
opened the window wide and looked up ; and there,
passing over the house and flying at a great height,
was a heron ! That was what the robin was

watching.   I spoke in my prettiest bird notes, and
told him he was quite safe in my neighbourhood ;
but no ! till the bird was out of sight he watched.
Then, in a moment, he was all hunger and confi-

ROBIN WATCHING HERON

dence again.   Perhaps he thought it was a hawk,
although the size and motion and everything were
so very different from a hawk's.   Perhaps it had
been taught to fear all large birds.   For that
birds, besides learning from the example of their

parents, are definitely taught by them, I feel sure.
I had thought that herons did not eat small birds ;
but Miss L. tells me she has seen a heron eat a
sparrow, feathers and all ! She thought it must
be choked, but it was not.

DYING NIGHT

WINDS of the dawn, melodiously sighing,
Sigh softly on, for gentle Night is dying!
Grey grows her face, the pale lids slowly fall,
And white mists shroud her, like a funeral pall.

Her patient stars are stealing from the sky,
Her owl flits far away with mournful cry,
Her ghostly blooms close up their honied store,
And tempt the downy haunting moth no more.

Softly her children slumbered on her breast
Farewell for ever to that sheltered nest!
Farewell the tender folding of the arms
That kept them safe from perils and alarms!

No dreaming more for them, for, cold as snow,
The bosom of the earth receives them now.
Therefore, O winds, sigh on with mournful swell
Farewell, O gentle Night!   Farewell, farewell!

CHAPTER VIII

March 14, 1886.

A LONG and trying winter this has been for both
feathered and unfeathered bipeds. To-day it seems
colder than ever, and the ground is so hard that
the strongest beaks can make but little impression
on it. A peewit has been strolling about on our
lawns, and I hear of many others, and also of
snipe and other unusual visitors. We have had
but little of the vast visitation of snow that has
buried half the world this year, and slain its
thousands of sheep upon the mountains of Wales
and Scotland, and not a few poor shepherds and
others.

My loss has been a bed of yellow crocuses.
Two days ago they were beautiful, and the
admiration of every one who came to the door.
Suddenly I perceived one morning that there had
been what seemed a miniature tornado in the
midst of them: the blooms were torn off and
scattered on all sides, and also torn to pieces. I
watched long before I discovered the malefactor in
a very large thrush that I had seen hopping about

the lawn a good deal lately. There it was,
gobbling up the beautiful golden petals as a rabbit
' tucks in ' lettuce leaves ! Not content with the
full-blown flowers, it tore the nascent buds out of
their sheaf of leaves, and even pulled up one crocus
by the root. Since then I have several times seen
it feasting there, and I know it is the same bird
by a small white feather in one of the wings. It
seems an old bird, and its movements are slow ;
perhaps from starvation ; perhaps—as I think I
have heard—there is something narcotic in the
crocus. I frightened the bird away twice, but it
was of no use, and now all the yellow crocuses are
gone. It has still left the white and lilac ones,
and I am curious to see whether these will be
spared much longer. It has not come to my
window, although I see it at times looking up at
the birds feeding there. I should send it away
(with a blessing) if it did come, as I keep very
select company at my window this winter, and
will have nothing to do with the large birds. This
is for the sake of my two tame robins, who were
with me all last summer, and have been here ever
since. I have also six blue tits, two cole tits (one
with a spot on her forehead, whom I call Spot), a
hedge-sparrow, and occasionally a nuthatch ; this
last, however, I do not encourage. The robins call
me when they want food, and sit close beside me,

and look up into my face in the most friendly
manner. The cock is especially confident. He
has a particular phrase of his much-varied music
for me. The robins know my voice and come
when called, and like to be talked to. They catch
one's eye too, in a way that I do not think the
other birds do. The cole tit's eyes can scarcely be
seen ; they are so involved in black : this must be
a protection to those delicate organs, always first
attacked by another bird.

June 14, 1886.

Winterly weather still ; though we have had
touches of mild summer. My robins and cole tits
are as faithful to me as if they had little to live on
but my scraps of bacon. But they have raised a
good many young ones, and those want feeding.
Just now a cole tit called me to the window (it
has more voice now) and when I appeared with
food, it was followed by a flock of little ones—of
two ages, I think. One lovely little thing, evidently just out of the nest, sat a long time on
the verandah, and was fed there. Its colours are
lighter and brighter than those of the older birds.
The white patch on the head and that on the
cheek are bright and large ; the black very deep
and glossy, but only above the eyes, while that
under the chin is scarcely perceptible : the back is
a lovely grey green, and the bars on the wings well

marked. The sweet little fluffy thing paddled its feet in the rain in the gutter of the verandah, and tried to sip some up. The old birds were very fussy, and much excited, calling the young ones with quite loud notes, and carrying off beak-loads of bacon, of which they seemed to eat but little themselves.

A thrush has brought up one brood in the garden, and is now sitting again, this time in the Pyrus japonica.

1887.

This year the tom-tits claimed my hospitality again, and I had no cole tits. They do not seem to be able to associate even to the extent of feeding at the same window. On the other hand, the robins have been there continually, and also in and out, feeding on my easel. I am beginning to think that it is jealousy and greed, and not affectionate discipline, that make the old robins so anxious to prevent young ones from sharing one's favours. The old robin has been curiously careful all the year not to come in when the young one was about. However, the young one found its way into the dining-room below, where also I had put food for it.

Two blue tits became very tame, and towards the autumn were always to be found hovering about the window when I came down in the

morning. They hung upside down on the sides
of the window, and shivered their wings at me
with pretty little cries of delight and expectation
—expectation which was speedily gratified with
little bits of bacon. Thomas and Thomasina are
a lovely pair, and their ways are charming. The
hen is very small; yet I think not young, she is so
very wise.

My garden this year was privileged. Notwith-
standing that there was building and garden-
making going on near me, I had a golden-crested
wren's nest in the juniper, two thrushes' nests one
after the other, and a fly-catcher's nest. This last
was built in the first empty thrush's nest in the
clematis on the house. I felt sure that the fly-
catcher must be building in that nest, though it
carefully avoided entering the clematis exactly at
that point. In the autumn I had it taken down,
and, true enough, there was the flycatcher's nest
within that of the thrushes.

March 7, 1888.

I am rather miserable about my robins. The
young robin has taken possession of the drawing-
room window now that the lower one is shut, and
it drives away the old one so savagely that the
poor little thing is frightened to death at it, and
will not come till it feels sure that young Bob is
not at hand. Sometimes when, after long listen-

I

ing, he comes to that conclusion, and hops up to
me and looks up into my face, and I open the
window and talk to him, and feed him—in fact,
just as we are quite comfortable together—down
comes that young brigand upon him like a thun-
derbolt, paying no attention to my presence, and
away goes my poor old friend, with the young one
after him, and I am left lamenting, and so cross
that for some time afterwards the young one
receives nothing from me but a scolding. In fact,
I think he has come to the conclusion that what
he is to get he must seize rapidly. Yet I have not
the heart to chase him away entirely; he is the
roundest robin I ever saw, and very handsome and
bright-eyed. He is very short-winged and short-
tailed, and splendid in colour; but his boldness
distinguishes him quite as much as anything else.
I saw him defy a nuthatch once, a bird that is a
subject of alarm to all the others, and one that,
for that reason, I do not encourage. Bob Junior,
however, does not molest the blue tits; he seems
to consider they have a prior right here, and the
gentle little hen I spoke of lately used to feed close
to him with the greatest confidence, holding a little
bit of bacon down with her foot, and pecking
quietly at it till it was all gone. But a little while
ago she had a fright; the robin came down on
her suddenly just as she was going to feed—put

his face close to hers, and glared at her as if he
was going to peck at her eyes. I saw them
become fixed and glassy; she seemed horrified—
paralysed; she evidently felt that it was all over
with her, and could not move. I came immediately to the rescue, and the robin flew away. But
she did not. She could not move for some time,
and since then she has avoided Bob. Her fear of
him shows itself in another way too. Not having
much voice to call me with, as her mate does, she
hit some time ago upon an ingenious plan of her
own for doing so by means of a rather prolonged
series of little taps with her beak upon the woodwork of the sash. She cannot reach the glass, but
when she has tapped, she rises on her toes, as it
were, and looks in to see if I am coming, or flutters
against the glass. This she has done for some
time now, and has found it very effective; but
since the fear of the young robin has fallen upon
her she has almost abstained from tapping lest the
sound should bring him up. Two little taps are
as much as she ventures on generally now; and
they are quite enough if I am there. She is a very
wise little bird; there is no doubt of it.

One very curious observation I have made
whilst watching the pair of tits; a very sugges-
tive one on the interesting subject of *origins*. The
two seem very much attached; they generally

I 2

appear together; but the hen always waits till her mate has fed. She sits on the rose-tree till he flies away, and then comes and takes her share. He, nevertheless, begins to feed without first calling her if he happens to come alone. On the other hand, if she comes first and begins to eat, and he arrives just after, he comes fussing and grumbling and angry. She gives place to him in a moment, but does not fly away. No; the curious part of it is that she stands aside, with her head carefully turned so as to look *away* from him, fidgeting all the time with unsatisfied appetite; but not till he has finished, and flies away, will she look in that direction! I remember observing the very same thing with a pair of nuthatches that used to frequent the window at one time, and have watched these proceedings often enough to feel sure that they would occur again under the same circumstances. In both cases the female was a good deal smaller than the male, yet it did not appear that they were in the least afraid of their husbands. No; it is not fear. What then is it? It seems to me that it is an incipient feeling of etiquette or decency. That is a feeling that must have a very ancient origin in animal history. It is probably the consequence of a feeling of *unprotectedness*—of exposure to danger during certain actions—which is the original cause

of their being accomplished apart from others.
Animals are shy while eating because the head is
bent, the mouth and eyes are engaged, and a
sudden attack would find them unprepared ; hence
the custom, and from custom has come etiquette.
The origin of drinking healths, of *pledging* each
other when drinking, is, I believe, something
similar. When men wore dangerous weapons and
feuds were common, a man who raised a flagon
to his lips for a long draught, hiding his eyes
and engaging his right hand, was exposed thereby to a stab from any enemy who happened to
be at hand, and therefore a friend pledged his
word to protect the drinker. Hence the custom,
and etiquette.

March 20, 1888.

Snow and cold winds continue.

LET the cold snow lie still. Lie still, cold snow !
Ye sunbeams, touch it not, but leave it so ;
The worn and weary earth sleeps well below—
    Lie still, cold snow !

Her flowers had budded and had blossomed fair,
And decked her bosom as with jewels rare ;
Then came a quick sharp wind and laid it bare—
    Sleep, flowers fair !

They budded, blossomed, and were withered so ;
They bare no fruit ; but do not let them know :
Deep be their sleep beneath the sheltering snow—
    Let them not know !

We have diligently fed our birds, and kept them alive and in fine feather. Strange to say, not one of my yellow crocuses has been eaten this year, though thrushes are continually about the lawn. The taste of that old thrush must have been peculiar; or he may have been suffering from some disease for which he had been recommended to take yellow crocus!

The swallows will be late this year, I think, for the south of Europe seems still buried in snow. Talking of swallows, I remember recording, some years ago, how I watched for some time the feeding of some young ones on a low roof, and how very irregularly the old bird did it. I have come to the conclusion that it was my presence that disturbed her on that occasion, for I watched a similar scene last year, and was astonished at the regularity and impartiality with which the old bird performed its task. I watched for some time, and she never made one mistake, though sometimes several minutes must have elapsed before her return with another fly. At last, however, another swallow, the mate, I presume, came with a fly in its mouth just as she was feeding one bird, and put it quite in order into the beak of the next. This seemed to disturb her very much; she sat down (so to say) beside them, and began to chatter and twist about as if to reproach the other.

Perhaps it was to express confusion, or perhaps she was asserting the claim of the next on the row. At all events, when she returned next time, she evidently remembered all about it, and gave her fly to the right bird.

The old robin comes more frequently now, though the young one is as fierce as ever against it. Can this savage fellow be the child of the other?—one of those for whom he laboured so successfully last spring? I am afraid it is only too likely, or the little brigand would not feel so much at home here.

I had but one robin's nest in the garden last year, and that was the work of a foolish and pretty young pair that built in some ivy close to the gate, and within reach of the eyes and hands of all the school-children who pass to and fro twice a day. Unfortunately I did not see it till too late—not indeed till the young were out of the egg—or I should have removed it. One day I heard the click of the gate, and saw boys running down the lane, and went at once to see if a catastrophe had happened. There was an empty nest, and one poor little unfledged robin dead on the ground. The others appeared to be 'peeping' and piping and struggling among the shrubs in the next garden; but as they could neither walk nor fly, no doubt they perished.

The old robin was more successful. It built
its nest in the hedge on the other side of the road
going up the hill. The boys found it out, I believe,
for Mrs. Halse overheard them talking about it,
and I suppose they thought it better to leave
the young until they were fledged. But the old
bird was too clever for them. She must have got
them out of the nest very early one morning,
before they could fly, and managed to get three of
them, at all events, into my garden, under the
gate, I fancy. She knew no doubt by experience
that it was a comparatively safe place. On passing
a gooseberry bush near the gate that day, I
observed a tuft, or rather a small thick layer, of
withered grass on the top of it. Thinking it
looked untidy, I raised it, and was about to throw
it away; and behold! there was a dear little round
speckled thing under it, with bright surprised eyes,
looking up at me from the very middle of the
bush! wondering, but quite still and not afraid.

Of course I replaced its cleverly and carefully
prepared shelter, and took care not to let it be
disturbed. The old bird could hardly have devised
a better fortress for the little thing, the youngest,
no doubt. It remained there two days, I think.
Two others were stumbling and cheeping about
the garden for some time; one took an awkward
flight into the kitchen window.

The young pair, after sitting for a day or two
in a melancholy mood on the gate or near it,
gazing at the spot where the nest had been (for I
had removed it), went further afield for their
second home, though they came to the window
occasionally. Whilst they were feeding their
first brood at the gate, they used to come backwards and forwards constantly from them to the
window, feeding their young with the bacon which
no doubt slipped very comfortably down the little
throats. They came flying straight to me when
I came down in the morning, and seemed to hear
my voice across the lawn when I called them.

March 21, 1888.

Why putting the head on one side should be
an inquisitive gesture, I really cannot say; but
certainly the robins do it as well as their human
'superiors.' This young robin, who is not sure of
being always in favour, because I have sometimes
scolded and sent him away baconless when he
has been chasing my old friend, comes now with
a tentative air, stands beside the plate with his
head well on one side, and looks up in my face.
The expression of inquiry, which is of course
solely the effect of attitude, is quite perfect and
unmistakable. Is it an accidental coincidence?
or do others of the lower animals express inquiry
in the same manner?

CHAPTER IX

February 1890.

It is long indeed since I recorded anything anent my birds; not because they are at all less interesting to me, but because, naturally, the small incidents of their little lives repeat themselves, and there are but few perhaps that have not been observed and noted either here or elsewhere.

Nevertheless, I have been noticing lately something very pretty that I had not before observed. Two little cole tits have been waiting on me for some months past, till we have become excellent friends. They are quite familiar with me, and flutter in my face confidently and closely (the glass between, though), and hang on to the sides of my window till they must know the contents of my room almost as well as I do myself.

This little pair is a much-attached one; if one of them comes, the other is sure to be at hand, and to appear before long. The rule is that the cock bird, which is much larger and more strongly marked, and more masculine in manner, should

come and eat first, and then the little hen takes
his place. She is curiously small, and seems as
light as thistledown, and her wings quite cross
over her back; there is something distinctly
feminine and infantine about her ways. Perhaps

COLE TITS

that is why the other (Tit-willow I call him) is so
careful of her. Careful he certainly is, as the
incident I am about to relate will prove *to any one
who will believe it* ; it is likely enough that no one
will do so who has not seen it, and that is why I
send no account of it to 'Nature' or the 'Selborne

Society's Magazine.' I, for my part, have seen it
several times, and feel no doubt. If Tit-willow
comes, and finds that there is but one piece of
bacon left, he will fly to the little wife sitting on
the rose bush close by, and urge her to come and
take it ; and the way he does this is very curious.
The beak supplies the place, it appears, of both
fingers and lips ; he darts it towards the food, and
then towards her. If she still lingers, he goes
behind her, and darts his bill at her again, but I
think without touching her ; I have even seen him
apply his bill to the place where the ear is, or
should be, but I heard no sound. This was done
when she seemed exceedingly unwilling to go ;
she was, I think, afraid of a robin that she saw
about to come, and that he did not see ; for as
soon as the robin had gone, she came immediately.

Birds are much more human than any one
knows who does not watch, as I do, a few tame
ones *at home*. Their gesture-language is so clear
to me now that I fancy I can understand what
they are feeling, and what they are thinking so
far as it *is* thinking, as easily as if they could
speak. I can see the balance between the instincts of fear and hunger gradually shift in the
case of new-comers ; and watch the gradual in-
crease of cordiality, or at all events of tolerance,

between them and the old *habitués* of the window-
sill ; and I think I can trace in some of them a
growing perception of my countenance, as distinguished from my dress and general appearance.
This, however, may be fancy, except in the case
of the robins. It is the privilege of Bob to understand the human eye and gesture, to say nothing
of the voice, the tone of which all animals understand more or less.

I had a tapping tom-tit till lately, but alas ! it
has vanished. It used to come and press its little
yellow-green bosom against the bottom of the
glass of the window, holding on with difficulty by
the woodwork, and peck gently and look all about
in the room for me till I went to feed it, when it
would take up a waiting position on the very tip-
top of the highest rose-twig it could find, and
then let all the others feed before it came itself.
It seemed as if it tapped for the good of the community ; strange to say, though they seemed glad
to have the service performed for them, they never
tried to do it themselves.

After being nearly all day at the window, the
little tapper vanished suddenly, and I fear will not
return now, and the birds find it difficult to make
their presence known. One tom-tit has taken to
turning over the fragment of a broken water-colour
palette on which I put their food : he does it very

noisily, and I think it may be meant to remind me
that it is empty. How the little thing does it I
cannot think, unless it is by pecking hard at the
inside of the edge. It is a large blue-cap : they
differ much in size and colour, as well as in
character.

The little hen cole tit has a deal of quiet wisdom
in her comparatively large head, and this seems to
serve her instead of strength in maintaining her
place among the larger birds. Apparently she has
economical propensities, for she carries away more
than any of the other birds ; it is more than she
can possibly eat, and she must needs store it
somewhere. The male bird never does that ; he
feeds and goes his way.

January 1891.

The hen cole tit mentioned in the last paragraph
still remains with me ; but I have come to the
conclusion that her propensity is acquisitive rather
than economical. She cannot be said to store
that which she takes away, for she carries each
little bit of bacon to a separate place, and, as far
as I can see, pays no further attention to it, and
probably forgets where she placed it. That she
cares for its safety at first is plain from the skip
and twist and sharp look-out that she gives to see
that no bird is in the way likely to snatch it from
her.

Mrs. Brightwen, in her charming book ' Wild Nature Won by Kindness,' speaks of the cole tit as storing food, and I have seen the same assertion in another book about birds. Still, unless a store has been found somewhere and traced to the bird, I think it must be a mistake. The male bird does not even carry it away, except to a place where he can eat it comfortably.

I am grieved to record the death of Tit-willow. He was found lying dead on the top of the wall lately, and so it is his poor little hen who has to wear the willow! At first she did not seem to miss her mate ; but one evening it seemed to strike her that she had not seen him for some time, and she sat upon the rose-tree and piped for him in a most plaintive way, looking anxiously all about her and in amongst the branches of the rose, as if she thought he must be hiding somewhere. Since then I do not think her motions have been quite so lively ; but she carries off the food, and flutters and hangs about the window, as much as ever.

The tapping tit has returned, or another has taken to the habit. I think it must be the same bird, he is so very much at home, and so masterful. Very lame he is too ; he shakes his wings at me most lovingly and gratefully, particularly since he has been treated as an invalid. He appeared for some time with one poor little leg tucked up in the feathers of his breast, and staggering about on the other in a most painful manner. He has now nearly recovered. I suspect a chaffinch of having given him a vicious peck on the thigh.

There is a curious blackbird about here just now. It has a broad white band all down the back from the head to the tail, and when the wings are raised it is evident that the white feathers cover a great part of the back. It is by no means beautiful, and I think the other birds are rather shy of it.

The robins were curiously tame and sociable last summer and autumn, and still, when I *do* get out, they come to meet me. If I stoop to look for violets or anything, they will sit in a bush close by, and warble softly in my ear almost. Quite a whispered song it is, so soft and sweet ! If one did not see the little thing's throat moving, and its eyes fixed upon one, it might easily seem to be a bird at some distance to which one was listening. There were three little robins brought up in the rose bush close to my window, and it is probably those that are so sociable ; but I have heard of their singular tameness this year in other places. Their confidence is not misplaced, for they seem in high favour. I hear of no catapulting this year ; and it is said that a butcher-boy is in the habit of putting a little bit of meat on the

post-box opposite, as he passes, for a robin that
lives there. I hope I may flatter myself that my
'leaflet,' the address to boys and girls published
by the Selborne Society, may have helped to pro-
duce this pleasant change.

Many larks have come down from the snowy
hills, and pick up every bit of green food they can
find—cabbages, parsley, everything. They do
not seem to take any of the various food that is
put out for the other birds; but I have not tried
them with grain of any kind. Two were picked
up dead in the garden.

WINTER SUNSHINE

O GENTLE winter sunshine, slant and pale!
  Thy timid smile falls sweetly on the earth,
  And warms the poor chilled Singers into mirth—
The Poet, and the Robin on the rail.

Pale winter sunshine, weak as infant's touch,
  No marvels wilt thou work while thou art here;
  And though we feel thy power to charm and cheer,
When thou art gone we shall not miss thee much.

No rose will open its warm heart to thee,
  Nor Earth at thy demand yield up her fruits:
  The hidden ferns around the beech-tree roots
Will not unfurl thy pallid gleam to see.

The sleeping crocus buds will still sleep on,
  And willows wave bare branches o'er their tomb;
  But thou, athwart the leafless forest's gloom,
Wilt gleam where summer sunshine never shone.

CHAPTER X

December 21, 1876.

I AM very much amused with the birds on my window-sill. There were no less than five blue tits feeding there just now. So many do not often remain amicably there together. They maintain their feeding-ground against all comers, even chaffinches. This morning a robin had a fight with one of them, and though it at first conquered its little adversary and had its feed, it was driven away at last by a tit that flew straight at it. I fancy the tits' beaks are very sharp and strong.

By-the-by, I saw a flight of blue tits chased out of a spinney of larches not long ago by the long-tailed ones—it seemed by mere force of noise. Apparently the blue ones could not bear the shrill whistling any longer, and away they flew in a body. Perhaps they felt that in that case the bottle tits had a prior claim to the feeding-place.

March 26, 1877.

I am more and more impressed with the resemblance between birds and children: in both the motive of every action is evidently a mere balance of instincts. The blue tits are, I suppose, courageous because there are so many of them. Two or three together seem afraid of nothing, and even one will feed quietly on the sill when I am quite close to the window, provided it can keep a window-bar between my eyes and its own—just like a baby that hides its head when it is shy, or an ostrich hiding its head in the sand. After all, in each case, it is the fear, and not the danger, that has to be got rid of.

May 29, 1877.

I have had such a pretty little pleasure lately. A pair of goldfinches have built a nest within two yards of my staircase-window, on a bough of the sycamore-tree which I planted myself, but which is now higher than the house. It is nearly at the extremity of the bough, and swings to and fro to such a degree when there is wind, that I am almost afraid they will have to abandon it again. It is just in the draught between the two houses. Yesterday the wind was very violent, and though I saw them go out and in then, I have not done so to-day. Indeed, I have not seen them at all; I hope nothing has happened to them. Anyhow, I have had the pleasure of seeing them build it, and it was a pretty sight, for what do you think they built it of?—*lauter Blumen*! At all events, as far

as I could see, they fetched nothing else at all
but the long blossoms of the sycamore and the
long sprays of the forget-me-not. A more perfect piece of protective mimicry could hardly be
imagined. Looking up from below, it is scarcely
possible to make it out from the tree and sky.
The window, of course, they did not reckon upon,
as it is never opened; the top is covered with a
blind, and the lower part with flowers in pots. I
am afraid though that the passage to and fro of
lights at night (if they happen to open their little
eyes) will amaze them very much; and O, when
the wind blows, how that cradle will rock! The
babies are certain to fall out unless the eggs do it
first. The cradle is firm enough, and seems part
of the tree. It was so pretty to see them pop out
of the nest and flutter down upon the forget-me-
nots with a childish cry of exultation, as if they
had found them afresh each time. One waited
on the rail and looked, unless the worker (the
male, I suppose) found it very difficult to find
the right piece or get it off, and then it joined
him but did not help. Perhaps hers was the
little head I saw moving so rapidly within the
nest, weaving it in and out; or does the male
both fetch and build? Then they danced and
sang over it so! Sometimes they reminded
me, I am sorry to say, of ballet-girls dancing

and weaving wreaths, and waving them about
before building a bower for the heroine or
première danseuse; for the long blossoms were
not managed without a good deal of graceful
agility on their parts. [I add here from the note-
book the sequel to the story of this goldfinch's
nest.—Editor.] The birds' delight, which was
even greater than mine, was an artist's delight, I
feel sure—that which an artist feels in beginning
a new picture, or the delight so well described by
Jean Paul Richter of a young man who has an
idea and is going to write a book. An artist,
indeed, is apt to feel, as one of them (Orchardson,
I think) has said, that he is 'always beginning
the good picture and finishing the bad one.' But
with these little artists it was all rejoicing from
beginning to end, till the eggs were laid; and then
a quiet, patient, but still animated little head
could be just seen above the thickening foliage.
When I looked at the nest from below I could
see nothing of it; but, alas! the little artists had
not been so careful to guard against the eye of an
enemy overhead. One day, after the birds had
been for some time sitting on their eggs, and I
was looking forward to feeding the young, a terrible
catastrophe happened. I was at work at the
other end of the garden when I heard a loud
screaming and fluttering in the sycamore-tree,

and, looking up, I saw a large black creature fly
out of it. Whether it was a crow or a jackdaw I
was not near enough to see, probably a crow, for
they abound here, and it must have been large and
powerful enough to carry away the eggs whole,
for there was not a vestige of one in the nest
when I next looked. The birds too went. Late in
the year the branch was cut off, and the remains of
the dead flowers were still hanging upon the nest,
which I have.

April 27, 1878.

Do not *all* birds imitate to some extent? If
not, this is curious. I watched a cole tit singing
and hopping about close to my window the other
day in a rose bush. I learnt its note by heart—
a triplet, rather wiry, and one emphasised higher
note at the end. Next day I heard it again on a
tree and went to look, the cole tit being rarer here
than the others, and lo, it was a blue tit doing it!
I watched it for some time. It exerted itself
more than the cole tit, and the note was perhaps
rather less loud; otherwise it was exactly the
same, and I heard the same thing to-day. Now
I know perfectly well the notes of the blue tit;
it has several, but they are not like that. Was it
imitation? I believe I heard a starling doing it
the other day—at least, I could see no other bird
near, and it was louder than usual.

May 5, 1878.

Birds are very delightful, but I have almost blinded myself to-day watching flocks of fly-catchers and golden-crested wrens, &c., in the trees by the river; the leaves being scanty at present, it was almost like looking at the sky, which was bright, but more white than blue. But O, the pretty little dears! they seemed more in the air than on the trees; sometimes quite dangling in it from nothing at all. And I believe I saw an instance of another kind of imitation. I had been just watching a yellow wagtail wagging away on the stones in the river, when I saw something wagging on the tree above. Strange, I thought, for they never seem to settle on trees; so I looked nearer, and it was, I believe, a flycatcher *rigorously* wagging as the yellow wagtails do. Children and monkeys are imitative; why should not birds be? I have heard a robin give a capital singing lesson to another. It was most interesting to watch the pains the old bird took to set its copy, and the young to copy each little stave. They did not mind me, so intent were they.

December 29, 1881.

Did I tell you what a very clever starling there is here? I think not, though he has been performing all the autumn; now and then he adds

to his accomplishments. I may have told you
that he imitates the laugh of the woodpecker

STARLING.

(yaffle), for that he did last year; but now he
(I call it he because he does it in such a masterly
way) sits on a neighbouring chimney-pot just
about the time when the dinner is cooking, like a
priestess of Apollo on her tripod, inspired no
doubt by the fumes and warmth below; and there
he holds forth. First comes the laugh, as if to
call attention; then the blackbird is imitated—so
well that if you did not see the bird you could not
believe it was a starling; then the twittering of
swallows, then the warning note of the robin, the
croak of the rook, and once I think I heard the
quack of a duck. There can be no mistake about
the others. And the bird seems to enjoy it so.
' Er brüstet sich,' as the Germans say, and stands
as if on tiptoe, and turns his head from side to
side with the most absurdly affected and self-
satisfied air. He takes great pains; and in spite
of his airs and graces is quite absorbed in his performance. One would think he had an audience
before him of all the birds in the air, but generally,
he has only before him the wide expanse of earth
and sky from which to draw inspiration. Sometimes one sees another starling sitting a little below
—his mate, I suppose—looking up at him with
evident admiration; and I have now and then
suspected that he was aware of me and my admiration in the garden below.

Some starlings seem to remain here, but I think large flocks come and go also, passing south, I suppose, and returning.

The birds at the window are curiously numerous and tame this year, considering how warm it is. It may be in consequence of the absence of berries. I have not seen a holly-berry this year.

May 25, 1882.

How I wish birds ate slugs! I am afraid they do not. I am not sure about starlings. Do they? Bless them if they do! I never had so many young birds in the garden before, and O how amusing they are when they come to learn to feed on the window-sill! It is the swallowing that is the difficulty with young birds evidently. I have watched many young chaffinches being taught to feed. They soon peck a bit up, but cannot swallow it without assistance. I have been laughing aloud at a young chaffinch to-day; it pecked up a long bit of bread, and of course could not manage it, but was for all that quite determined to hold it against all comers. And so it did; with its back to the window, and the piece of bread for a lance, it defied them all, putting its little head down, as if it was going to fly at them. A number of birds came—sparrows, chaffinches, and even a nuthatch; but it held its ground and its bread, and they did not peck it. At last, when all had gone, another nuthatch came and pecked at it, and sent the little thing away, bread and all. It is the child of the old tame chaffinch.

The other day a fine blackbird flopped suddenly down on the window-sill. He was bold and eager, looked me all over, and evidently thought nothing of me, though he was close to the window. He packed his beak as full as he could, and proceeded to feed a young one that was sitting crying for food, on the edge of the verandah, and then away they both went. Presently I was recalled to the window by the clattering of the plate on which I put the bacon, and there I found the hen blackbird at work. She took every fragment that she could stuff into her beak and tried a long time to get in more, and gave a wicked stab with it, all the same, at a poor chaffinch who wanted his share. She evidently 'looked before,' and knew that when she came again the plate would be empty, as it proved to be. Then her instinct was at fault; for she seemed to think that if pecked and stamped and stabbed at long enough, the plate would at last yield up more bacon. She flapped and danced and stamped and tugged till at last she dragged it off the sill, and away it went, down the verandah roof and on to the lawn. The bird flew away, very much alarmed——' the bird

ran away with the dish.' Plate unbroken, and
bird soon feeding from it again as if nothing had
happened.

Can you tell me what bird it is that utters a
delicious liquid, long-lingering ' glou-glou,' loud
and clear and slow, from the top of a tree? I
thought it must be Hebe, pouring out amber
nectar into crystal vases for the gods in the sky;
but it was a long-winged brown bird, rather
larger than a cuckoo. I could not get a near
view of it, and only heard it twice; it was very
delightful.

June 23, 1882.

I have lost my tame robin; and it was so
tame! — perhaps it will appear again, but there are
such flocks of chiffchaffs and flycatchers about in
the garden that the timid little thing may be
afraid of them. It seemed so very shy of birds.

No doubt I am related to the birds through my
grandmother, who was devoted to them and kept
a roomful; and I always was Jenny Wren, and
wore a brown gown, and would not go too fine.
Nevertheless, I think that the real reason why
birds are so tame with me is that I go softly and
alone.

December 8, 1882.

I have quite a flock of birds every morning
now at the window: one nuthatch—such a funny,

bold, inquiring bird—hangs on to the sill and stares me full in the face, moving his great head and beak from side to side, a pair of cole tits, three or four pairs of blue tits (O, so fat and so pert and busy!), and sparrows and chaffinches without end; but the robin 'remains out,' as the Germans say. I cannot get the robins to come and feed with the other birds, though they do watch their opportunity and come sometimes. But they are the tamest of all the birds in the garden, and also I think the most thoroughly musical. I had a duet with one the other day; it was just above my head in a bay-tree. I sang to it, ' Robby bob—bob—bo-o-o-b!' and it answered immediately; then I, then Bob; and so on, ever so long, till I was tired. The bird evidently enjoyed it, and hopped about looking at me as if it had half a mind to come down upon me. The cole tits are very confiding, gentle, graceful birds; but they do not seem to take so much notice of one.

The starling that I mentioned as having a talent for mimicry has been imitating the thrush lately admirably. I was quite puzzled one day to know which it was (for the thrushes have been singing a good deal), and so went to look for it, and watched it for a long time. It was giving its performance evidently with immense satisfaction to itself, sitting on a chimney-pot with its head on one side, and its feathers all abroad.

December 23, 1883.

I do not feel sure that I am writing sense, for the robin is most distracting. He is very tame, comes when I call him, and can stand almost any disturbance. Having finished his breakfast, he thinks of the future, and guards the plate. The way he does it is most comic. If a bird comes down the robin darts at it, even if it be a nut-hatch; and while on the watch he twists first one way and then another, and then dances a little, always with the head on one side, as if he were deaf with one ear and listening hard with the other. Away he goes, and the others come. Well done, hedge-sparrow! it has sent two chaffinches to the right about.

But a little while ago, a valorous tom-tit flew violently upon a nuthatch that was feeding quietly alone, and actually made it shout out and fly away. Very courageous these tom-tits are!

Back comes Bob—clucking, and very angry to find the crumbs gone.

April 10, 1885.

Fancy Mr. Morris not knowing of the presence of the nuthatch in Devonshire! I have written to assure him of the fact. [To the note thus sent Mr. F. O. Morris wrote in answer :—' There is no doubt from your accurate description that your birds are the nuthatch, and I will enter the place in my interleaved copy for any future edition, and will mention your name in connection with it.'— Editor.] They seem to me very numerous ; but, then, so are high trees, and no one looking from this window would think we were near the sea. I have heard of a lady here who had six nuthatches that visited and fed at her window. I had two of them, and two robins, a blue tit, and a cole tit, all at my plate together yesterday. I wish Mr. Morris could have seen them ! They do not always endure each other's company so peacefully, but I was there to see fair play, and they knew I should do so.

My robin pair come together now, and carry off, instead of eating, neat little bits of bacon carefully chosen. They dart round the corner into the orchard, where I conclude sitting is over, and several young throats are gaping for food.

April 24, 1885.

When one sees a small bird chasing a large one, as one often does, I think we may safely conclude that the larger bird has stolen an egg or something from the small one (unless it is a hawk,

then I think the little birds fly after it by way of
' keeping mischief before them '), and that, having
its mouth full, it is unable to peck.

It is curious how much more confused the
instincts of a robin are than those of a tom-tit,
though the robin is the more human of the two.
Here comes one with its beak full of food for its
young, but it wishes to pack in a piece of bacon
too. Then another robin appears below, and off
goes number one to dance to it, food and all—the
baby for the moment forgotten. Very human !

December 10, 1885.

I have two robins, three blue tits (' Yes, Bob,
I'm coming ! '—he is continually calling me to
feed him), and two cole tits, who are always expecting to be fed. The two robins fight, but the
robin does not fight the small birds. It is pretty
to see a blue tit, with its quicker wings, steal a
bit of bacon flung to the robin, and then fly round
the robin's bewildered head as if it were laughing
at it. The cole tits always wait till larger birds
have filled their beaks ; then they come with
perfect confidence. I have positively to fight with
the old chaffinch to prevent it from eating everything up. I do not encourage the nuthatch ; I
am so afraid for my robin and dear small tits.
They are such companions ; but they make me

L

open the window oftener than I should, though
only for an instant.

August 17, 1886.

I find my opera glass (euroscope) of great use
in bringing the birds within watching distance;
but it is curious how quickly birds find out that
they are being watched. I do not think there is
anything they fear so much as an eye; and, by-
the-by, it occurred to me the other day to wonder
whether the eyes on butterflies' wings might not
be, for that reason, slightly protective. I assure
you, as I was watching one of those brown butterflies with eyes on their wings the other day, I
felt just as if the thing was looking at me through
them. And to-day I noticed a small moth (dark
orange bordered with black, I think) with eyes on
it that had two very small specks of white on
them which exactly answered to the reflected
lights in the eye; those sparks, mysterious to the
ignorant, that used to be taken to be the soul
itself. Some have three great eyes on each wing
staring at one. If I were a bird, I am sure I
should be frightened at them.

November 28, 1886.

My uncle John was a great lover of birds.
He not only had a good collection of stuffed birds,
and of books on them—Gould's magnificent folios,
Bewick's, &c.—but also an aviary full of gold and

silver pheasants, cockatoos, parrots, &c. Before
him his mother was devoted to them, had a room
given up to them, and kept nightingales in song
through the winter, and an overpowering noise they
made. They had list on their perches, were
wrapped up at night, and were fed with meal-
worms, chopped egg, &c. This love of birds is a
passion which has, I think, descended to me and
to some others of our family. Uncle John could
imitate the nightingale's note so exactly that I
have seen, in the twilight of evening and our
shrubbery, a nightingale fly down to him, and
almost strike him in the face as it passed. We
had birds among our ancestors, no doubt. I used
to be told when a child that I was like a robin.

That young robin has come back ; not quite so
tame, but I think it is the same. It flashed past
me the other day as I stood at the window, and
took refuge in the darkest corner of the room, an
angry parent after it. It comes for its breakfast
as regularly as a certain tom-tit. The ways of the
two are comical in the extreme, or rather the tit
is comical. The robin's ways are graceful, and
pretty, and lively, and insinuating. I never had
so bewitching a one before.

June 30, 1887.

I am very birdy still. Robins have been
hopping in and out of the room all day, carrying

off bacon for their young. And there is such a piping and peeping of young birds! Two broods of young thrushes have been brought forth in my garden (and now they are eating all the strawberries, quite unripe!——ungrateful things!). Then there was the brood of missel thrushes hanging over the road, and some dear goldencrests built in a small juniper. Though the tree was so small, and the nest within reach of my hand, and I could watch them fly out and in, I never could see it till the birds had left, and I could pull the boughs apart, so cleverly had they hidden it. It could be seen though, I suppose, by sharp eyes, for I was standing at the window one day, and I saw a butcher's boy, as he passed under the tree, all at once put down his basket and *go for it*! Fancy my horror and the energy of my deprecation! I soon made him understand that was no business of *his*. I have been in a fright about it ever since, and was glad to hear them all uttering very lively miniature pipings last Sunday in a way that showed they were ready to be off; and so they were, early next morning, and now one hears them all about the limes and Virginian cedars. It is not altogether a pretty note, like scissors rather, but the wee things are so pretty, one likes to hear it. The nest is most curious. I took it down when I was sure they had done with it. It

is like a cluricaune's cap, with the opening below.
All the dirt had accumulated at one spot on the
lower edge, so evidently the birds must have clung
inside the hanging nest. Did you ever see one?
I knew they hung.

The flycatchers that built in the clematis are
gone; I do not feel sure whether they got their
young away safely. If, as I believe, they laid
their eggs in the old thrush's nest (they were in
it, or very near), it was so accessible that I fear
they may have lost their eggs or their young; at
all events they came no more. The thrushes' nest
in the black-currant bush against the garden wall
had a curious fate. The young birds were looking
very wise and nearly ready for flight one morning
when I went to look at them, and soon after the
old thrush was heard to scream out by Mrs. H.,
who took no notice. When I next went, after
dinner, behold the currant bush had broken away
from the wall, and the nest was almost upside-
down, and, of course, empty. The nail and string
had given way. I searched in vain for any young
thrushes, but they must have got away safely to
M.'s shrubbery, as I soon heard them cheeping
sharply there. But one was, as usual, weaker
than the others, and that one, I think, must have
been left behind concealed under the rhubarb
leaves; for two days after we found it under the

long wire defence that I had put over the late-
sown peas, and which joined, with an opening, on
to the rhubarb. It could not walk, but had
scrambled to the other end ; and there it lived on
very contentedly for three days, the parent coming
to feed it. I put a rhubarb leaf over it, and
thought it a very nice safe place. So, I suppose,
did the old bird, or she might have got it out by
the way it went in. She herself had been caught
there a short time before, and made a fine fuss.
I had to let her out.

The young pair of robins that lost their brood
by the gate have come back now with another
well-grown family, and I think the old robins
have two broods about ; any way there are a great
many of them, and I am very glad of them.
What should I do without the birds and roses !

August 19, 1887.

I think the little straddle-legs you ask me about
must be a young robin ; but it must be a very
young one for picking up crumbs at a window. I
am afraid it must have lost its nursing parent, or
it would not be allowed to do so. I have a theory
that one parent takes two nestlings under its
charge, and the other another pair, and that they
keep apart. I may be wrong.

The flycatchers are very busy here just now,
snapping and twisting about ; they have to be

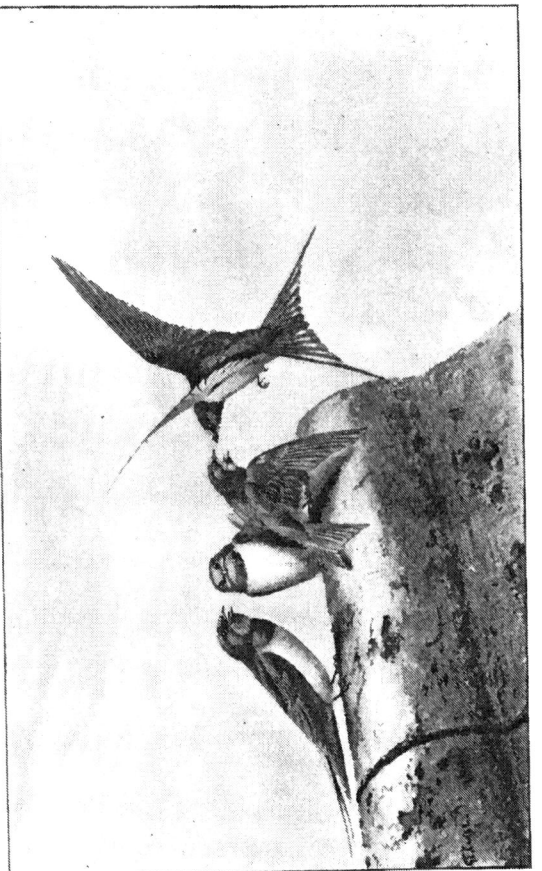

SWALLOWS

quick to follow the rapid evolutions of the winged
things they feed on. The other day, after a good
hard shower, they were tumbling about in the
strangest way on the grass, pursuing the insects
that had been *floored* by the rain.

Do you remember my letter in ' Nature ' about
the six little swallows having their dinner, in
which I had to remark that the parent fed them
very indiscriminately, and by no means each in its
'turn? Well, the other day I watched the feeding
of two, on a high roof above human interruption,
and I was amazed at the regularity with which
the bird gave each a fly in turn as it passed ; and
that too though several minutes must sometimes
have elapsed before it returned. I feel sure it was
one bird ; for once, just as she had popped a fly
into a little beak, the other parent flew by, and
put one into that of the other ; whereupon the
first parent, instead of flying off as usual, settled
down beside the one it had just fed, and began to
chatter. Perhaps it meant : Be so good as to go
back to your own charges, and do not interfere
with my proceedings ; if you do, I shall forget
which to feed next. Perhaps it was making a
note for future use that *that* one was to be fed
next, although it had just fed it. Any way, everything went on as before, and the right bird had it
next. I waited to see if it would be so.

November 19, 1887.

Tom clings upside-down to the window, and asks to be fed. He manages, when I am very inattentive, to get up a miniature squeak. I am sure he would do more if he could; and it is curious that a creature that will have a fine loud, clear, thrilling call about two months hence, should be so dumb now.

CHAPTER XI

IF I did not talk to the birds my jaws would grow stiff. The tits have grown quite imperious. Tom scolds loudly, hanging above my green curtain, till I go to him, and then he shakes his wings with delight, and goes to fetch his wife, if she is not pecking at the window below. She has taken to doing that very often and loudly: is it for want of a call? But I believe it was she who the other day sent forth quite a sparkling fountain of little silver notes as I looked at her. She is so much smaller than Tom that I could not be mistaken. Tom sings too at me if the scolding does not succeed: a loud trill it is, and quite irresistible. But they waste my time dreadfully.

March 18, 1888.

Did I tell you that that small hen tit had taken to tapping at the window for me? at the woodwork; she is not tall enough to tap at the glass, but she jumps up and looks to see if I am coming afterwards. She woke me up tapping at my bed-

room window one morning at seven o'clock. She
could not have known I was there, and was probably trying windows in general. She is very
wise for her size.

May 13, 1888.

Two sweet young thrushes' heads are peering
out of the nest in the yellow jasmine on my wall,
and so far I have prevented them from being
taken ; though I caught the bookseller's youth one
day, with his hand burglariously threatening the
nest, and his feet among my flowers, and I have
had a bird-stealing mason in the house. Oh, the
birds are so funny just now ! My two tits impe-
riously demand to be fed with bacon still, but the
cock feeds the hen now and then as if she were
a young one ; and she puts on such ridiculously
infantine airs, and emits such baby croakings from
her open mouth. The next minute she is feeding
herself as cleverly as ever. Can it be a game of
play ? Do they play at nurseries as we did at
houses ? The robins do the same. I'm puzzled.
Poor old Bob goes about without a tail. Has he
pulled it out, do you think, to adorn his nest ?
Or has some dog or cat grabbed at it ?

May 15, 1888.

The birds certainly have an æsthetic faculty
both for sweet sound and brilliant colour. I wish

you could have seen my tame cock robin one day.
He was *very* shabby himself—almost stripped—
moulting, I think, and so was his wife. I had been
bewailing their condition for some time, and so
had they ; the cock looked piteously at the place
where his scarlet and white ought to have been,
and seemed quite humbled and low-spirited.   He
was standing so on my verandah one day, having
bits of bacon thrown to him, when suddenly there
alighted on the window-sill a fine young robin
—the handsomest I ever saw—and in perfect
plumage. You should have seen my bird!—he went
off into the wildest ecstasies, flamed up with unmistakable admiration, and danced and sang and
erected his crest at her ; never was such adulation !
But she was quite indifferent to the poor little
shabby fellow, and quickly disappeared, he after
her.

Both my robins are about now constantly with
their two fast-growing and extremely hungry little
ones : they never seem to bring up more than two
here.

March 27, 1889.

One of my tits, who has learnt to tap for me,
hangs on with his feet to the bottom of the window,
and tries to catch hold of the glass with his wings.
Such a scratching he makes !

May 26, 1889.

I was quite wrong in supposing that the robins had lost their brood. There are three young ones about in the garden, and as only one of the old ones is in attendance on them, possibly a fourth may have gone off with the other parent. They do divide their forces in that way I know. Three are too much for one robin to feed ; even with the assistance of my almost constant supply of bacon, the poor thing looks worn to a shadow, a bag of bones and feathers rather. I believe I, mainly, am bringing up three large families (one of robins, one of blue tits, and one of cole tits), to judge by the great packets of bacon they carry off in their beaks ; and in such a hurry ! The blue tit was in such a flurry yesterday that it came in to see about supplies, and then could not get out again ; so I had to catch it and put it out.

It is curious how different the cleverness of one bird is from that of another kind. Glass never puzzles the robins ; but this old and very clever blue tit, that has fed here for years (I believe), cannot see it or find its way out. Several times I have had to release a blue tit from the window. The cole tit is wonderfully intelligent (it is almost all head and legs, so it ought to be !), but it dares not venture in. And yet it has not a speck of fear outside, and carries off larger packets of bacon

than the robin even, and so curiously well-packed.
It has no *fear*, but it takes good care not to
encounter a larger bird than itself, and never
comes till the others have fed and the coast is
clear of them.

One of the little robins (a very fine bird) is
wonderfully tame. I made its acquaintance
whilst digging up some ground for a new violet-
bed. It came up confidently at once (its mother
did not know, evidently, —or—), pecked about,
examined my boots curiously, looked up at me to
see the connection, walked in and out of the prongs
of my fork, and found a good-sized slug, out of
which it proceeded to peck the life, and also part
of the substance. I did not know that so small a
bird would eat a slug. It could not manage a
worm, and pecked shyly at a woodlouse. It is
always about the kitchen door, and if I turn up
earth in the garden it is nearly sure to come and
see about it. It eats moderately of bread, but is
always friendly to my maid and a great resource
to her.

It seems wonderful that with a dog on each
side of the house the old robin should have been
able to keep these three little feeble fluttering
things out of harm's way; but the ingenuity it
shows, and the terrible anxiety it sometimes
undergoes, must be seen to be believed. *The*

hiding-place is under the rose hedge, amongst the
thorns and weeds ; twice I have found a heap of
dry grass laid over where the small thing had been
placed (I knew the meaning of it from having once
found a young robin hidden under grass in the
midst of a gooseberry bush), but now she ventures
to feed them in the oval bed in the middle of the
garden. Here there are generally two together,
but sometimes one joins its elder brother, the little
gardener, in the back garden ; sometimes they
fight, and sometimes they flutter off, and she loses
them. She had the smallest by her the other day
as I stood by the dining-room window, and, seeing
me, came to ask for something. I gave her some
bacon, and while doing so the little one slipped
through the hedge, and she could not find it. So
she put the bacon down in a safe place, and went
about looking for it, and the expressiveness of her
actions was something wonderful to see. Up and
down, and in and out she went, with growing
terror, and then began a soft low moaning sound
that I have often heard used on such occasions.
It seems attractive, but still little one did not
come, and she came to me, hopped up on the
window-sill, did not touch the bacon but looked
inquiringly into my face, asking as plainly as
possible if I knew where it was. I was obliged to
say that I did not : then it began again, and went

through into the next garden — found it, and immediately came back to fetch the bit of bacon it had hidden, and lured its child back to safety—to my relief as much as that of the bird. I should be grieved if anything happened to them.

July 14, 1889.

I think you must be the E. H. who writes in 'Nature' about flies and swallows. It is not only swallows, as of course you know, that suffer from parasites. About a month ago I was standing at my drawing-room window, when an old blackbird alighted on the lawn just before me, and began to twist and turn, and kick and scratch and peck in a most vigorous and remarkable manner, more especially towards the region of the tail. I thought the bird seemed to be hurt or in convulsions, and went to see if I could render any assistance, but it flew away. When I went back to the window, there was the bird again in the very same place, and doing the same thing; and as it did it, I saw quite a cloud of little gnats or flies rise from it. It rubbed itself so on the ground that I thought there might be something in the grass there that would help it, but the spot was like the rest of the grass.

August 8, 1889.

A tamish cole tit has just been here, asking for bacon and quite at home, yet it must be two

M

years at least since one has been here feeding.
Then a pair were constantly here, and brought
their young. Can this be one of them? I wonder.

August 27, 1889.

I am writing with the window open, and an
opera-glass at hand, for there is such a piping—
squeaking, rather—in the cedar opposite! Golden-
crests or very young tits; I should say the first,
only Thomasina came just now and clung to the
side of the window and asked for food (for her
young, I should think), which I gave her. She
seems very good friends with a handsome cole tit,
who also comes here now. They are almost my only
visitors at present; dogs and cats have abounded
so of late that the old robin keeps watch in the
sycamore and will not let the young ones come.
She dashes at them and drives them away.

I fancy the young males of the first brood are
learning to sing just now. At all events, there
are very queer snatches or phrases of song or
conversation to be heard. Very short and sketchy
they are. The young birds *are* golden-crests! I
caught sight of one in my glass just now—a fine
little kinglet; but they do flicker out so quickly!

December 11, 1889.

I had a curious visitor on Sunday. I was
feeding my tom-tits in the afternoon at the drawing-

room window, and rejoicing in the beauty of
Tom's new wife, when I perceived on the lawn
below, not far from the path, a very large bird
pecking and pulling at the grass, and staggering
or waddling about in a very strange manner, and
going backwards every now and then. On bringing my glass to bear on it, I perceived (as I had
thought beforehand) that it was a green woodpecker—a very handsome one too. I watched it
a long time ; it seemed dreadfully hungry, and it
evidently found great stores of ants. Presently a
girl came up the path with a note, and passed
close to it ; the bird took no notice, and when she
put her hand nearly on it, it just jumped away a
few paces and fed on. So by-and-by I sent my
servant down to see it, as she did not know
the bird. She walked up close to it quite
quietly, and it took not the smallest notice. My
curiosity was excited, so I wrapped up well and
went down gently to it, and stood beside it for
some time, admiring its red crest and wondering.
Then I put on my spectacles and stooped down to
look more nearly at the mystery, and behold it
was blind ! When my head was near, it felt something, and turned its head to bring the other eye
to bear on me, and then retreated a few steps, so
I think perhaps it could see a little with one
eye. I could not see that it had been wounded or

injured in any way, but its eyes were *glazy*. It
was fat, apparently, but birds look fat when they
are not so, and the poor thing must find it dreadfully difficult to find its food. No doubt that
was why it so steadily adhered to my ants' nests.
I have seen green woodpeckers at them before.

It went on eating and pecking and pulling for
an hour or more, and, indeed, only flew away
when it was almost dark.

February 6, 1891.

By-the-by, Mrs. Brightwen says that the cole
tit *stores* its food. I think she is mistaken. My
little hen cole tit, at all events—the little widow,
who with her late mate has been under my
observation for two or three years—does not *store*,
though she *takes away* incessantly till the plate is
empty. She looks round well first on both sides,
turning as on an axle, with a little skip, and
where she sees no bird near, thither she carries
her morsel, and lays it on any convenient branch
—on the point where a twig starts generally, and
apparently thinks no more about it. I have seen
her carry it quite to the top of one of these tall
limes. It is not an economical impulse apparently,
but an acquisitive one, and it appears to be her
strongest. The male bird never did it.

Are thrushes usually considered imitative
birds? I suppose they all are more or less so,

but the way in which a thrush here imitates the quack of a distant duck is marvellous. How does it arrive at such a low note? It also, *I believe*, imitates the squeaking and scrooping of an infirm wheel-barrow that used at one time to go up and down this road a good deal. It caught that up last year, but it has brought it out again now most emphatically and unmistakably. The thrush has not naturally a note like a wheel-barrow with a loose unoiled wheel, has it? I think I have heard it imitating a robin. Thrushes are numerous here just now, but blackbirds seem to have vanished. Perhaps they are offended or inconvenienced by the starlings, who are perpetually imitating them. *I* should be, I am sure: all the more that the imitation is so good.

June 20, 1891.

I think I told you of our imitative thrush. It has been away, or silent, for some time, but piped up again yesterday on the same tree-top. Just now it imitated the noise a hen makes when she has laid an egg so exactly that I could not help laughing. But the bird makes long pauses now between its performances, as if it were listening or trying to recollect. I think I told you it imitated the gull, but I find it was a peacock that it was imitating. It does it

admirably, only the size of the throat reduces the
cry till it is as like the cry of a gull as anything
can be. There is a peacock across the river, and
when that begins, I recognise the thrush's imi-

ROOK AND BLACKBIRD

tation of the cry. It is the loudest thrush I ever
heard.

The young robins and their mother have gone
away, and old Bob comes in and out again.

The blackbirds are very tame here. One was

feeding its young yesterday in the garden, and soon after I heard its alarm cry. On looking out there was a large crow of some kind sitting on the wall, looking out for young birds. So I clapped my hands loudly, and away went the crow, but the blackbird – close to it – moved not an inch. It watched the enemy well away, and then looked round gratefully at me—or so I thought.

That same bird sprang its rattle the other day on the appearance of M.'s black cat, and went on rattling for, I should think, half an hour, just behind Topsy as she sat on the wall watching for young birds.

The tits have vanished away to the woods at last. Two pretty flycatchers are doing good service over the tops of the roses, twisting and turning after the butterflies in the most wonderful way.

September 2, 1891.

We have had—and lost—two little tame robins; so tame that they followed me about, and into the house, and would eat out of anyone's hand. I hope they may come back some time, but I do not think it is safe to make robins so tame.

February 2, 1892.

M. has left me her robin to feed; fortunately he had become used to my window-sill before, and he feeds off my finger quite as confidently as from hers, and sings for a bit of bacon whenever he needs it for himself or his mate. She has it thrown to her—has, for months—but never will come up!

I have lost that dear little eloquent cole tit that had so much to say to me and that said it so plainly! My little hen has another mate, but we neither of us think much of him at present.

February 17, 1892.

Bob comes after a very timid hen that has been about here for months, but never grows more confident. She comes to the window, and utters a small 'peep!' but when I go she retreats to the edge of the verandah, and expects me to throw bits of bacon to her; and if there is a tit in the way she is sure to lose her bit; for she is slow, and has not the courage to dispute it. I think Bob feeds her.

May 4, 1892.

The little male cole tit has thrice eaten out of my hand lately, but 'timously,' as Mrs. Halse remarked, and only after seeing the robin do it. These tits do not mean to leave me yet, I see. They become more and more delightful and hungry, and now it is a pretty sight to see the two come together, the hen coquettishly asking to be fed by the other, as if she were an infant, and

could not do it herself! And the *empressement* and
care with which the male chooses a nice little
morsel, and puts it gently and tenderly into the
open mouth of the little quivering, squeaking
hen!

June 5, 1892.

I have only seen my robin once since my return; he saw me from afar at the window, and
flew up and took a piece of bacon graciously from
my hand, by way of saying that I was not forgotten; but he is feeding his young ones in M.'s
garden, and she feeds him most constantly.

My tom-tit came next day and all day; for,
finding things quiet and the window open, instead
of tapping as usual, he dropped in, looked carefully
about; and then found the plate under the desk,
and carried off a supply of bacon (to his family,
I suppose), and kept on doing this all day. He
made such a mess with the bacon that I was
obliged to put the plate elsewhere.

The chorus of birds is almost too much; the
whitethroats especially are singing incessantly,
and they overpower the blackcaps. One blackbird
is continually on the lawn, feeding a young one
that looks larger than himself.

June 13, 1892.

All the birds have forsaken me, except the
very timid hen robin whom we named 'Spectacles.'

She is as shy as ever, but comes in and out continually to a plate of bacon placed on the easel or table for her, and she evidently looks to me to put it there, although she does not like me to look at her, or speak to her. So unlike most robins!

M.'s Bob, the mate, we think, of Specs, is as sociable as ever, and comes to her directly she calls him. He has only paid me one visit. I think that, as usual, he takes half the brood about with him, and she the other. They must have three or four children, to judge from the amount of food they take away.

September 9, 1892.

My robin has grown so splendid; I see him sometimes sitting lost, apparently, in contemplation of his bosom. He trots upstairs now and then after Mrs. Halse, and comes constantly into the hall with me, and is quite affectionate. But an old robin tries to drive him away; and he gets behind me in the garden when he hears the old one coming.

December 28, 1892.

It is seldom I am able to go into the garden, but if I do, there is Bobinette who rushes at me, flutters about me with unmistakable delight till I reach the sea-kale pots, where she takes her expectant stand till I come up, and sometimes even after, till I have to ask for my seat. She is well

fed at the back door, and rather despises my little
bits of bacon : it is real affection on her part.

February 2, 1893.

How amorous the birds are becoming already !
I was amused with Tapping Tom just now. After
tapping most importunately (as he does when his
lady is there too) for food, when I put it out, instead of taking a bit or feeding, he settled on the
near branch of the rose-tree, and, turning his back
to me, began a quite peculiar little cry, looking
about in the meantime for his lady, who appeared
to have given him the slip.   How the little head
did twist and turn, to be sure !   All at once, down
he came on the plate (heard her, no doubt) ; but
not to eat ; off he went with a bit for her in his
beak.   M. says she often sees them feeding their
ladies on her lawn now.

Where, O where can the line be drawn
between the inherited and the acquired ?   Here,
for instance, is this blue tit, 'Tapping Tom.'   He
has *inherited* the knowledge that a certain call
brings that which he wants in the shape of a
mate ; he has also *acquired* the knowledge by
experience that tapping at the window brings me
and food.   The first piece of knowledge will pass
on to his progeny ; the second will not do so, I
suppose ; but where can the line be drawn between
the two kinds or bits of knowledge ?   Only the

manner of the acquisition seems different—not the nature of it. And the experience of the effects of an impulsive cry was probably the root and origin of the instinct inherited in the former case. My belief is that our language began with the expression of *feelings*, as does that of the birds and beasts; that it went on to express warnings, demands, and commands. So does the language of birds, as to the expression of warnings and demands at all events.

February 9, 1893.

Four rooks have been busy on the limes opposite this morning; not, of course, with a view of building there; the branches are not forked enough, and there are plenty of elms about; but they like to take the long flexible lime-twigs for making their nests.

February 27, 1893.

Old Tom taps more than ever, especially when his wife is with him. I know by the sound whether she is there or not (generally, at all events); and it is pretty to see how he takes a little bit, and then makes way for her and encourages her to come. But they *never* eat together. It evidently is not etiquette amongst birds for the two to eat together; at least it seems so with tits and robins.

May 3, 1893.

I saw the other day in a paper by 'A Son of
the Marshes,' an expression that was new to me.
Speaking of the songs of the different birds then
going on, he says, 'the yaffle yikes.' (Enter
Robin fluttering round my head with a large piece
of bacon in his beak, startled by something outside, I think.) To 'yike' is Norfolk, I suppose ;
did you ever hear it? We used to call its very
peculiar cry 'laughing '—a very appropriate name
for it. The yaffle used to be much more common
here than it is now ; I have seen three feeding
together on my lawn in the very early morning,
eating ants.

A pair of nuthatches used to come constantly
at one time, and brought a young one sometimes.
But I do not encourage them now, for I find that
the smaller birds are afraid of their large strong
beaks and rough ways. Sometimes a nuthatch
looks very funny from the window, hanging upside-down on the edge of the verandah, its tail
pointing skywards : one wonders what it is.
There is a squat reptilian look about the bird
that one does not like ; nor does one quite like its
relation to the butcher-bird.

September 10, 1893.

Bobinette came down to my feet to-day, but
a male Bob was singing loudly, and came down

to her and distracted her attention. One or the
other—or another—has been warbling a whispered
song deliciously in the rose hedge at dinner-time
lately ; twice it has done it, two days following.
I watched the creature quite close, but it turned
its back, and shook its wings and went on, so I saw
that the delicate attention was not intended for
me. There seem to be many robins about, coming
out into bloom and song. Perhaps we shall have
nests and eggs and young birds at Christmas :
such things have been here.

October 5, 1893.

Bobinette misses me in the garden, I hope :
the last time I went there she was sitting waiting
for me on the sea-kale pot. She did not at first
take kindly to a new coloured dress, but after
wandering suspiciously about the skirt, she jumped
up in the gooseberry bush, and stared hard at me
as if to say, 'I must learn well the part of her
that does not change.' Really that bird's face
was a study. Instead of the usual arch side-long
glance, it stared and squinted and blinked ; and
at last I believe it 'wunk,' as the Americans say
(don't you think we had better adopt some of their
strong preterites ?) I am sure it wunk. Since
then it does not seem to mind what I wear, and is
very dear and affectionate.

TO MOTHER EARTH

My Mother Earth, what will you make of me?
When on my tired bones your weight is laid,
What will you make of me, O Mother Earth?

Make not a rose—I was not beautiful;
Nor yet a violet—none called me sweet;
Let no forget-me-nots, with earnest eyes,
Make vain appeals to dulling memories;
And bid no yew nor cypress fling its shade
Upon my grave, for weary I shall be,
And glad to rest; nor yet victorious bay;
For, Mother Earth, there is not much of me,
And when I sang none listened. Listen now,
O skilful Mother! listen to me now,
And I will tell you what to make of me:
The purple heath that clothes the lonely hills,
The purple heath shall flourish from my bones.

For once, long years ago, one summer day
My mother and her friends together met
To celebrate a birthday festival;
And whilst their children sported in the sun
They talked the flower-language in the shade,
Then set themselves, making speech visible,
To crown each childish head with fitting wreath.
So one was decked with hospitable oak,
Mixed with the brilliant gladness of the broom;
With myrtle one, and one with passion-flowers;

One wore the rose, and one the jessamine,
And one the mignonette and pansy-flower.
But I was crowned with solitary heath,
And midst the purple bunches there was set
('That's for simplicity,' our mother said)
The single rose, thornless and evergreen,
The white Leonida.

          The warm day passed,
And all the wreaths lay dead save mine alone,
Which flourished still—a night-sky set with stars
For though the petals fell, the shining leaves
And golden stamens of the roses stayed.
Upon an ancient mirror it was hung,
And there remained for many and many a day,
And then it vanished—whither, who can tell ?

For me, I think it passed into my life,
And crowns it still ; for, single and alone,
I've trod a thornless path and colourless ;
Dreaming of beauty on the purple hills,
And listening to the music of the winds.
Therefore, O Mother, make a patch of heath
Of my old bones, a patch of purple heath ;
Not large, obtrusive ; let the grass grow too
For, Mother Earth, there is not much of me.

  August 27, 1882.

INDEX

PRINTED BY
SPOTTISWOODE AND CO., NEW-STREET SQUARE
LONDON

CPSIA information can be obtained at www.ICGtesting.com
Printed in the USA
LVOW05*1724060813

346585LV00008B/174/P